Promoting a Successful Transition to Middle School

Patrick Akos

University of North Carolina at Chapel Hill

J. Allen Queen

University of North Carolina at Charlotte

Christopher Lineberry

Charlotte-Mecklenburg Schools

EYE ON EDUCATION
6 DEPOT WAY WEST, SUITE 106
LARCHMONT, NY 10538
(914) 833–0551
(914) 833–0761 fax
www.eyeoneducation.com

Library of Congress Cataloging-in-Publication Data

Akos, Patrick.
    Promoting a successful transition to middle school / Patrick Akos, J. Allen Queen, Christopher Lineberry.
        p. cm.
    Includes bibliographical references.
    ISBN 978-1-930556-98-0
    1. Middle school education—United States. 2. Articulation (Education)—United States. 3. Student adjustment—United States. 4. Academic achievement—United States. I. Queen, J. Allen. II. Lineberry, Christopher. III. Title.
    LB1623.5.A424 2005
    373.236—dc22

                                                    2004030215

10 9 8 7 6 5 4 3

Editorial and production services provided by
Freelance Editorial Services
(845-471-3566)

Also Available from EYE ON EDUCATION

Dedication and Acknowledgements

For my beautiful wife, amazing daughters, terrific colleagues, and family and friends, your unconditional support will forever be appreciated. Special thanks to those school counseling graduate students at the University of North Carolina at Chapel Hill for your help and your dedication to learning and helping students thrive.

—Patrick

To my wife of 32 years, I would never have made the transition to college without your support and belief in me. Thanks to all of my doctoral students that assisted directly or indirectly with this project, may your transition to the doctorate be most successful

—Allen

To my son, Caleb, and to my parents and siblings, thanks, for never giving up on me and supporting all of my efforts to better myself professionally. To my friends, Ron, Christa, Brian and Michelle, without your support and assistance my dreams would remain just that, dreams. Thank you.

—Chris

About the Authors

Patrick Akos is an Assistant Professor of School Counseling in the School of Education at the University of North Carolina at Chapel Hill. Recognized as the American School Counselor Association's 2004 Counselor Educator of the Year, he teaches introduction to the school counseling, group work in K-12 schools, career development and educational planning, and clinical practice. Dr. Akos's research focuses on school transitions, middle school counseling, and Developmental Advocacy. Currently, his research continues on how school personnel can promote successful transitions between elementary, middle, and high school (and the assorted configurations found in school districts) and how school counselors can intervene and advocate for optimal development for early adolescents. More information can be located at: http://www.unc.edu/depts/ed/med_sch_counseling/faculty.html.

An educator for 10 years, **Chris Lineberry** received his undergraduate and master's degrees both from The University of North Carolina at Charlotte, where currently he is pursuing his doctorate in educational leadership. Chris has been an assistant principal in a middle school in an urban setting with 80% of students at or below the poverty level, an administrator in a magnet school of the arts in a large metropolitan district for grade levels 6-12, and a principal in a Pre-K through 8th grade school in the rolling hills of Richfield, North Carolina in the Stanly County School System. Chris and his son Caleb both reside in Locust, North Carolina.

J. Allen Queen is currently Professor and Chair of the Department of Educational Leadership at The University of North Carolina at Charlotte and has been a classroom teacher, principal, college administrator and university professor. He has been a consultant to over 160 schools and districts in 36 states and 3 foreign countries in the areas of classroom discipline, student transitions, block scheduling and time management. Dr. Queen has written over 24 books and 75 articles including books on karate for children. In addition to books, Allen has appeared on numerous radio and television programs, including *ABC World News Now*. Dr. Queen enjoys working with teachers and principals of block scheduling, student transitions and time and stress management. Allen has also worked with numerous universities, businesses, and government organizations in time and stress management. Dr. Queen was a major consultant for several years to the Justice Department in Washington as a presenter of the Attorney General's Selective Seminars.

Table of Contents

1

An Overview of School Transitions

It is evident that educators are aware of the importance of school transitions by the way each school seems to find an event to welcome new arrivals. Elementary schools have Beginners' Days for entering kindergartners and their parents each spring. Middle schools welcome field trips of rising sixth graders. High schools conduct open houses and registration nights for rising ninth graders. Many colleges and universities welcome new freshmen with a special seminar during the summer or a few days before the sophomores, juniors, and seniors return. And all educational institutions—be they daycare centers, elementary, middle, high schools, or universities—mark the transition of their graduates with pomp and circumstance. Students, parents, and staff celebrate with pride, smiles, and tears over leaving the past and fears about the future. Schools cannot function effectively without planning these ceremonial tributes to transition. The school community would not allow it. Although parents and educators may have the best of intentions, some students get lost forever in transition.[1]

A variety of interpretations exist as to the meaning of transition in the educational process. To some, transitions reflect a one-time set of activities undertaken by programs, families, and children at the end of the year. To others, transitions reflect ongoing efforts to link children's natural environments to school environments. Last, others define transition as the manifestation of the developmental principles of continuity, that is, creating pedagogical, curricular, and/or disciplinary approaches that transcend and continue between programs.[2] Kraft-Sayre and Pianta (2000) defined transitions as the process that all partners experience as students move from one level to the next, rather than a single event that happens to a child. Regardless of the focal point, transitions are increasingly being recognized as critical periods in the movement through public education in the United States.[3]

All schools, regardless of level, have a vested interest in improving the transitions of students both into and out of the institution, yet few schools offer more than a single transitional event for incoming and outgoing students.[5] The school community demands a ceremony, but the academic achievement and social-emotional health of students demand more.

Communication and Planning

Communication and planning are essential to all successful transitions, no matter what age, developmental level, or type of school. Communication must involve all relevant parties: the sending school or agency and appropriate staff, the receiving school and staff, parents, and students.[6] All involved parties need to communicate openly and honestly about their concerns, needs, and desires. Cross-level communication is neither common nor easy to accomplish.

What the Researchers Have Discovered

♦ Children who do not make effective transitions will be less successful in school, have difficulties making friends, and may be vulnerable to mental health problems.

♦ A child's transition to school creates a foundation for future academic, social-emotional, and behavioral development.

♦ Sixth graders show a statistically significant achievement loss after the transition to middle school compared with sixth graders attending K–8 schools with no such transition.

♦ Ninth graders entering high school experience academic achievement losses regardless of whether they attend a middle or K–8 school; those who attend middle school, and thus experience two transitions within a three-year span, experience even more severe losses.

♦ Students who experience a higher number of transitions are more likely to drop out of high school.

♦ A large number of students who drop out of school are of average or above-average intelligence.

♦ Many of the factors associated with dropping out of college relate to transitions from a non-middle-class lifestyle to a university lifestyle.

♦ Special education students at all levels experience academic and social difficulties in adjustment as they make transitions throughout their educational careers.

♦ Successful students have at least one adult who cares about their personal success.

♦ A sharp decline has been seen in the percentage of students who complete college, marry, start a family, and reach financial independence from their parents.[4]

Communication in Effective Transitions

- Developmentally appropriate involvement of and communication with students regarding their concerns and how those concerns relate to their future school setting
- Curriculum and program alignment across school levels, which requires communication between the sending and receiving schools
- Communication between the school and parents concerning curricula, school schedules and procedures, and developmental concerns[7]

Once communications have been established among all of the relevant parties, an effective plan for transition can be created. Creating effective communication and plans resulting from that communication can involve a great deal of time. Beyond the time spent planning, however, implementation of an effective transition can take the better part of the terminal year, with the cooperation of the sending institution.[8]

A Snapshot of Transition Issues

Kindergarten

Although developmental psychologists have written extensively on school entry, less research has addressed the overall effect of successful transition programs for kindergarten.[9] Most researchers have focused on the effects of transition on academic achievement, ignoring the broader ramifications of a kindergartner's first year of school on his or her social and emotional health. However, a growing body of research may provide guidance for educators as they plan and implement transition programs for incoming kindergartners.

Transition researchers at all levels have found losses in academic achievement as students progress through their first year in a new school.[10] At the primary level, researchers have provided educators with a strong rationale for the importance of continuity in the transition from early childhood to school-age settings. Academic achievement at the kindergarten level is widely attributed to early intervention programs; however, some researchers have shown these initial cognitive gains fade as students move through the primary grades. In the National Head Start Demonstration study, Bohan-Baker and Little (2002) suggested that local commitments to effective transition between local sites appear to combat the "fade-out effect" with respect to student achievement.[11] Additionally, Ramey and Ramey (1999) found that children who received additional environmental support as they moved into and through kindergarten and the early elementary grades performed better in reading and math.[12]

Some ingredients of a successful transition to kindergarten are completely within the control of the local school. Schools that create classroom settings that are developmentally appropriate, child centered, and well managed are more likely to observe successful transitions to the formal school setting. These successful transitions can then translate into an educational future that includes higher academic achievement, more prosocial behaviors, and improved attitudes toward school.[13]

Other ingredients of a successful transition to kindergarten require a broader base of communication and planning. Pianta, Cox, Taylor, and Early (1999) reported the key ingredient is the relationship created between home and school. These researchers suggest that frequent, regular communication between home and school creates trust and mutual responsibility for a child's educational development.[14] Kagan and Neuman (1998) suggested adding early care providers to the groups that plan and implement successful kindergarten transitions. They indicate that if schools communicate with daycare and prekindergarten schools regarding curricular concerns, students will be better prepared to make the transition to kindergarten.[15] Mangione and Speth (1998) provided evidence that broad-based partnerships among homes, schools, and the broader community can help to create effective kindergarten programs that ease transitions for children. They suggest that shared leadership and open communication can improve the process.[16]

Transition to kindergarten cannot be planned after the fact. A week after school begins may be too late. School is one of the most profound influences on a child's life, and, because kindergarten sets the tone for a child's entire school career, it is essential that successful transition plans be created and implemented effectively. Long-term orientation programs beyond the traditional Beginners' Day, such as home visits by teachers and other school staff and buddy programs with older students, have all demonstrated effectiveness with individual students. Each elementary school needs to find the right approach that fits each individual student and distinct school context.

Middle School

The topic of successful transition—both the transition from elementary school to middle school and the transition from middle school to high school—has become a topic of interest in education during the last 30 years. Students, teachers, and parents are all concerned about the transition from elementary to middle school. Students express concerns about getting to class on time, handling additional workloads, finding correct rooms, opening locks and lockers, drug use, office referrals, and ensuring personal safety.[17] Teachers worry about students' maturity levels, the effects of peer pressure, adolescent physical development, reduced parent involvement, and insufficient basic skills.[18] Parents worry about all of the above, in addition to the social concerns of having an adolescent child.[19]

Unfortunately, these all-too-real concerns often result in student losses in academic achievement and/or social-emotional well-being. Specifically, Mullins and Irvin (2000) found that student motivation decreased with the transition to middle school, as did academic achievement in English, math, science, and social studies. Students who were chronic truants or aggressive and disruptive in elementary school became even more so after the transition to middle school.[20] Diemert (1992) discovered that students' perceptions of the quality of school life in general declined after the transition to middle school.[21] Fenzel (1991) found that relatively young girls of lower socioeconomic status are even more at risk for problems during the transition to middle school.[22] Certainly, the transition from elementary to middle school can be a negative turning point for children.

Middle schools can take proactive steps to minimize these problems by devising programs at the middle school to ease the transition from elementary school. Teachers can deemphasize the importance of ability and competition in their classroom assignments. They can provide more group work, with an emphasis on effort and improvement. Teachers can also provide students more choices to allow for greater autonomy.[23] Middle schools that utilize interdisciplinary teams also find fewer transitional problems and improved academic achievement when compared with middle schools that departmentalize.[24]

Other steps to ease the worries of transition from elementary to middle school require more vertical communication and interaction between schools. For example, students who experienced some level of teaming and changing classes in elementary school reported fewer concerns about middle school than those who did not. This suggests that planning to ease transitions to middle school must involve students, parents, and staff from both the elementary and middle schools. By establishing activities, timelines, and evaluation procedures for the transition program, all parties can discover critical information about responsibilities and curriculum.[25] Weldy (1991) found four critical elements in a successful transition program: communication, cooperation, consensus, and commitment.[26] Jones (2001) collected a series of possible activities that could be coordinated between an elementary and a middle school, including a cross-school buddy system, middle school participant panel discussions at elementary schools, copies of the middle school yearbook and newspaper in the elementary school library, and open houses conducted in both the spring and summer to familiarize transitional students with lockers, locks, and class changes.[27] Cooke (1995) suggested that rising sixth graders have the first day of school to themselves, with older students arriving the next day. Without these efforts, students can easily be lost to truancy, antisocial behavior, and apathy during the middle school years.[28]

A Midwestern Middle School: Addressing Social Needs and Academic Concerns

♦ **In March**

Every fifth-grade teacher fills out an information sheet on each student. Data include reading and math ability, writing ability, counseling needs, home support, learning styles, student–student conflicts, and organizational needs. This is forwarded to the middle school counselors to begin the placement process.

♦ **In May**

The counselor visits each fifth-grade class to discuss different aspects of the middle school. Topics range from homework to scheduling to school activities and clubs.

♦ **In June**

The school sends a letter inviting all parents and students to attend an open house. The students and parents follow a schedule that allows them to meet all of the teachers in the sixth grade as well as tour the campus and see the school. Eighth-grade students volunteer as tour guides and answer any questions the students or their parents may have.

High School

The problems and concerns associated with transition from elementary to middle school can intensify with the transition to high school. Queen (2003), in an appearance on the *ABC Nightly News,* stated that ineffective transitions to high school have played a major role in the nearly 25 percent high school dropout rate in America.[29] Students are more likely to become apathetic about school as they move to high school, losing the sense of school belongingness and decreasing academic achievement.[30] Some students, drawn away by work or family and no longer interested in school, drop out and, at times, illegal drug use increases.[31]

Some of the factors that contribute to the increased sense of alienation among rising high school students may be systemic in nature. Students who transition twice during adolescence (once to middle/junior high and again to high school) are more likely to drop out and experience greater losses in academic achievement than students who transition only after attending a K–8 school.[32] Also, students who attend larger high schools are more likely to drop out than students who attend smaller high schools.[33]

Programs do exist, however, to help ease the transition from middle school to high school. The more extensive and comprehensive the transition program, the lower the subsequent dropout rate and ninth-grade retention rate.[34] The best programs include resources for parents and result in improved teacher–student relationships.[35] The School Transitional Environment Project (STEP) program,[36] in which ninth-grade teams are used to improve adult relationships with students, is one example. Quality transition programs begin early in the middle/junior high eighth-grade year and supply students and parents with high school information, provide students with social-emotional support during the transition, and bring middle and high school staffs together to work through curricular and procedural issues.[37] Counselors and social workers also play a major role in these programs.[38]

> ## Culbreth Middle School, Communities-in-Schools High School Transition Initiative
>
> Communities-in-Schools goals:
>
> ◆ Introduce students to high school while they still have the support of parents and middle school staff.
>
> ◆ Give parents a chance to discuss problems in small groups.
>
> ◆ Help students begin thinking about career choices and the role of the school in those choices.
>
> Communities-in-Schools process:
>
> ◆ One day a week (for six weeks) is dedicated to transition activities at the middle school.
>
> ◆ Students spend one morning in the spring with a high school mentor, with whom they tour the school, attend classes, and learn about extracurricular activities.[39]

College/University

Family and societal expectations of college attendance have risen over the past years, to the point that fully two-thirds of all graduating high school seniors attend college. Unfortunately, many students find themselves unprepared academically (and socially-emotionally).[40] Approximately 50 percent of students who attend college drop out before completing a degree.[41]

The greatest determinants of how and where students go to college remain family socioeconomic status[42] and other demographic factors over which schools have no control. However, schools can help to promote factors associated with college success. Students who take rigorous and progressively more challenging coursework in high school are more likely to succeed in college. Mathematics preparation is particularly important: Students who take algebra, geometry, and other higher-level math courses in high school are more successful in college. These course-selection patterns begin as early as the eighth grade.[43] Thus, curricular planning and consultation between middle and high schools and colleges can help to ease the transition burdens for students who continue their schooling.

Students who go to college directly from high school and attend full time are more likely to complete a degree. Students who delay entry or attend part time are more likely to drop out. Although the decision to delay entry or attend college part time is associated with family income, high schools with knowledgeable counseling departments are better able to advise students and their families of these facts.[44] Borgen (1995) reports that high school counseling departments can help all students, college bound or not, to develop multiple plans of action following high school graduation, to learn to advocate for themselves, and to manage changes in relationships with peers and parents. Borgen suggests high school counselors develop work and secondary education programs to help students acquire the skills and experiences that help with preparation.[45]

It is clear that as students grow older and parents make fewer decisions for them, a strong and knowledgeable middle and high school counseling program can help to prepare students for the transition from school. However, the reduction of parental influence does not mean parents are no longer important participants in the transitional process. Middle and high school counselors engage students in educational planning and career development. They also help students to crystallize college choices and provide intensive information and guidance. Counselors then follow through with all students to provide both information and support and to ensure that students access important information and attend college preparation meetings, take entrance exams, and complete admission requirements. A strong working relationship between counselors and supportive parents is extremely helpful.

Once students choose and are admitted to a college, that institution takes over the transition process. The most common transition programs involve orientation strategies. The programs provide descriptions of college course offerings, expectations for students, information about various assistance programs, and encouragement to establish working relationships with faculty.[46]

Unlike transition programs for elementary, middle school, and high school, there is limited research on communications between the sending and receiving schools in the transition to college. Milton, Schmidtlein, Mintrop, MacLellan, and Pitre (2000) explored the lack of policy coherence between K–12 and higher education. They found the current disconnect between the two groups may be the result systemic education efforts taking place at the K–12 level. Their research indicates that current K–12 student assessment efforts do not assess college preparation. They also discovered frequent misalignments between what is taught in high school and college admission placement procedures. These misalignments contribute, in their view, to the number of college students in remedial courses and to the high dropout rate from college. Milton et al. also discuss the major difficulties in bridging these gaps, especially considering the number of colleges that may receive a single high school's graduates.[47]

Exceptional Children

School transitions raise a variety of issues for the exceptional child. According to federal law, services for students with disabilities begin when a child is three and continue until the age of 21. Several problems arise as students enter exceptional children's programs, including a lack of planning for services prior to the child's third birthday and not including a school district representative in planning sessions. There are similarities between these problems and those occurring as students enter kindergarten. Planning cannot begin after the fact, and appropriate personnel must be included in the planning sessions.[48]

As exceptional students enter middle school, appropriate planning between schools is often an issue. Gallagher (1994) found that the elementary records of students forwarded to the middle school did not provide receiving teachers an effective assessment of students' current performance levels.[49] The Individual Education Plan (IEP) often does not provide sufficient information on the student's achievement level or competencies. Work samples and test results should be discussed, ideally, among the sending and receiving teachers before the child arrives at the middle school.

Additionally, many special education students coming from the elementary level are placed in inclusion classrooms and regular education classes with minimal or no support. The middle school setting is totally unlike the elementary setting, which is generally a resource classroom with a low teacher–student ratio. Those who prepare the IEP and make placement decisions should consider the transition problems that can occur between elementary to middle school. Placements should allow for an adjustment period and provide students with adequate support.[50]

The problems associated with transitions intensify at the high school level. Unfortunately, youth with disabilities are no exception; research has shown these students have higher dropout and unemployment rates than their nondisabled peers.[51] To address these problems, in 1990 Public Law 101-476 (Individuals with Disabilities Education Act) mandated systematic workplace-transition planning for these students beginning at the age of 14. Unfortunately, this law does not mandate attention to special needs in the transition from middle school to high school. The law defines these transition services as a coordinated set of activities for a student, designed with an outcome-oriented process. These activities, which include vocational education, integrated employment, continuing adult education, and independent living in the community, are designed to promote successful movement from school to the postschool environment. Studies have shown the dropout rate for exceptional students has decreased since the law was implemented in 1990.[52]

Tillman and Ford (2001) suggested that educators consider the following when transitioning exceptional students to life after high school: The ultimate goal of IEPs is to prepare students for their life in the community; educators should have proper knowledge of community agencies that provide training and services for disabled adults; curricula at the high school level should be functional and integrated; most importantly, students and their parents should be involved in the planning, implementation, and follow-up of IEP and transition plans.[53] Properly executed, these plans should enable exceptional students to become responsible and contributing members of the community.

Summary and Looking Ahead

As transitions become critical closing and opening rituals for students, developmental pathways are significantly influenced. The chapters ahead focus specifically on the transition to middle school. Chapters 2 and 3 discuss both individual development and the environmental or contextual changes that occur in transition. Chapter 4 highlights some of the major research findings and themes that all practitioners should be familiar with. Finally, chapters 5 and 6 provide research-based and practical suggestions for transition programming, including a variety of examples from schools around the country.

References

1. Queen & Algozzine, 2005.
2. Kagan & Neuman, 1998.
3. Queen & Algozzine, 2005.
4. Alspaugh, 1998a, 1998b; American Sociological Society, 2004; Gallagher, 1994; Gladieux & Swail, 2000; Jewett et al., 1998; Kagan & Neuman, 1998; Perry & Weinstein, 1998; Queen & Algozzine, 2005.
5. Kagan & Neuman, 1998.
6. Borgen, 1995; Ragan & Neuman, 1998; Ramey & Ramey, 1994; Smith, J.B., 1997.
7. Borgen, 1995; Chapman & Sawyer, 2001; Mangione & Speth, 1998; Mizelle, 1999; Kagan & Neuman, 1998; Waggoner, 1994; Weldy, 1991.
8. Kagan & Neuman, 1998; Lindsay, 1998; Shill, 1987; Waggoner, 1994.
9. Jacobson, 1998; Perry & Weinstein, 1998.
10. Alspaugh, 1998a; Perry & Weinstein, 1998.

11. Bohan-Baker & Little, 2002.

12. Ramey & Ramey, 1994.

13. Perry & Weinstein, 1998.

14. Pianta, et al., 1999.

15. Mangione & Speth, 1998.

16. Kagan & Neuman, 1998.

17. Akos, 2002; Akos & Galassi, 2004; Arth, 1990; Schumacher, 1998.

18. Akos & Galassi, 2004a.

19. Akos & Galassi, 2004b.

20. Mullins & Irvin, 2000.

21. Diemert, 1992.

22. Fenzel, 1992; Queen & Algozzine, 2005.

23. Anderman & Midgley, 1996.

24. Mullins & Irvin, 2000.

25. Alspaugh & Harting, 1997; Arth 1990; Waggoner, 1994; Weldy 1995.

26. Weldy, 1991.

27. Jones, 2001; Queen & Algozzine, 2005.

28. Cooke, 1995.

29. Queen, 2003.

30. Isakson & Jarvis, 1999.

31. Berliner, 1993; Catterall, 1995.

32. Alspaugh, 1998a, 1998b.

33. Alspaugh, 1998a.

34. Hertzog, 2002.

35. Smith, J.B., 1997.

36. Felner et al., 1997.

37. Mizelle, 1999.

38. Chapman & Sawyer, 2001.

39. Chapman & Sawyer, 2001.

40. Borgen, 1995.

41. Brawer, 1996.

42. Science and Engineering Indicators, 2002; Shill, 1987

43. Gladieux & Swail, 2000.

44. Brawer, 1996; Gladieux & Swail, 2000.

45. Borgen, 1995.

46. Brawer, 1996.

47. Milton et al., 2000.

48. Colorado Department of Education, 2001.

49. Gallagher, 1994.

50. Gallagher, 1994.

51. Patterson, 1996.

52. Mitchell, 1997.

53. Tillman & Ford, 2001.

2

The Developmental Transition of Starting Middle School

The transition from elementary to middle school represents a rite of passage for many youth. The movement into adolescence has itself been labeled a turning point or transition, with potential for great promise as well as numerous problems. With no formal rite of passage into adulthood, the stage of early adolescence is often seen as the formative struggle from childhood to adulthood. With the exception of the first 18 months of life, students experience more changes between the ages of 10 and 14 than at any other time in their lives.[1] The significant individual developmental changes that occur, in combination with the transition from elementary to middle school, have important implications for school personnel. Many attribute the challenges associated with the transition to middle school to two major and simultaneous changes: pubertal change and school change.[2] This chapter highlights aspects of pubertal change and facets of developmental change that occur for most students moving from elementary to middle school.

Early adolescence is a qualitatively distinct developmental phase. "The adolescent is often portrayed as impulsive, out of control, confused, self-absorbed, rebellious, violent, alienated, and involved in drugs, alcohol, and unremitting sex."[3] This negative view of early adolescence in popular culture causes many adults to lower expectations or be pessimistic. A look at traditional developmental theory in early adolescence helps explain and clarify some of these perceptions.

Traditional Developmental Theory

Physical Development in Puberty

To understand the developmental change that occurs during transition, it is useful to examine traditional stage theory for development in early adolescence. Although the timing varies, perhaps the most noticeable shift that distinguishes elementary school from middle school students occurs in puberty or personal-social development. Consider for a moment the tiny sixth grader who is pushed aside during the scurry between classes, or the young, womanly appearance of a 12-year-old girl. Through the squeaking early adolescent voice, we also hear the deep-toned threats from the mature eighth grader, strutting through the halls, defiant and rebellious against the authority of teachers and administrators. These obvious distinctions between students illustrate the effects of puberty.

Puberty brings a growth spurt that includes reproductive systems, increased weight and height, and other novel physical changes (such as pubic hair and voice changes). Vernon (1993) highlighted the consequences of such changes, including struggles with coordination and the impact of self-perception and other perceptions. Students, especially girls, are often in the midst of physical and hormonal change during the transition to middle school. This time of rapid transition also has little pattern or structure. This specific human development sequence does not follow a set timetable. Because the rate of physical maturity varies, it can be one of the most difficult periods of development.[4] No two students will experience the same degree of growth and development—a fact that creates an interesting challenge for school personnel. Eccles (1999) reported that early maturation tends to be advantageous for boys as they participate in sports, seek social recognition, and move toward the male cultural ideal with increased muscle mass. Alternatively, it can be problematic for girls as they experience menstruation, gain body fat, and encounter heightened scrutiny from peers. Although girls' feelings about development can mediate outcomes, early-maturing females tend to have higher rates of depressive symptoms and report lower ratings on body image.[5]

Growing early adolescents require time and energy to get accustomed to their new bodies. Puberty brings awkwardness, uneasiness, and pressure to maintain a positive self-image. These young students feel constant pressure to gain acceptance through their appearance, which often results in mood swings, bullying, and frequent changes in opinions.

Early adolescents feel as though they are on the world's stage, constantly being scrutinized by peers—an "imaginary audience" thought process that generates a great burden of stress.[6] Think, for instance, of the preteen who stops in every bathroom to check her dress and hair, or the boy whose speech is muffled all day by a hand that is covering an unsightly pimple or braces. Students such as these feel under a spotlight, open to ridicule and harsh peer interaction. This audience gets more intense as early adolescents discover intimacy and the opposite sex, which raises the pressure to gain acceptance and attraction. Likewise, as researchers have posited, the onset of puberty coincides with a rise in sexual harassment.[7]

Data on the transition to middle school have demonstrated that synchronous changes in puberty and school transition can be detrimental to coping abilities.[8] Because girls often experience puberty before and during the transition, they may be at particular risk. Research has demonstrated that the timing of puberty rather than pubertal status itself is associated with depression for early-maturing girls.[9] School personnel need to be sensitive to physical development and its potential implications during the move to middle school.

Identity Development

Students in elementary school may begin the process of self-awareness, but in middle school students use this knowledge to establish a sense of identity. Ask most middle school students to describe who they are, and you will be answered with a blank stare. This time of exploration and contemplation also comes with situations that create pressure, strain, and confusion. Beyond differences in the rate of physical development, consider that a middle school student may become the butt of a cruel joke or elevated to a higher social status by landing a date with the school heartthrob. Throughout the day, an early adolescent may ride a roller coaster of emotions that engender a wide range of thoughts, behaviors, and reactions. Parents and educators will sometimes witness drastic changes in appearance, opinions, and moods in early adolescents as they attempt to form their identities. "One day you come home to find him meditating in the lotus position, the next he's trying out for the football team. Two weeks later, he joins a rock band, yesterday's role cast aside as easily as a dirty pair of socks."[10]

Erikson highlighted these triumphant and tumultuous years, where struggles center on the psychosocial aspects of the child's life and, in particular, the exploration of independence and the concept of self. He viewed early adolescence (ages 7–11) as a time of exploration and identification of talents and capabilities. Contending with increased peer competition, youth fear being left behind or judged as substandard. Erikson characterized this period as the *industry vs. inferiority* psychosocial stage. Children either gain competency in new skills, or they feel inferior and unable to perform successfully. As one may suspect, lacking success at this stage of transition can trigger negative feelings toward school, teachers, and friends, as well as low self-esteem.

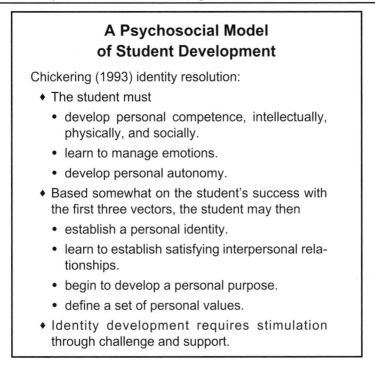

A Psychosocial Model of Student Development

Chickering (1993) identity resolution:

♦ The student must

- develop personal competence, intellectually, physically, and socially.

- learn to manage emotions.

- develop personal autonomy.

♦ Based somewhat on the student's success with the first three vectors, the student may then

- establish a personal identity.

- learn to establish satisfying interpersonal relationships.

- begin to develop a personal purpose.

- define a set of personal values.

♦ Identity development requires stimulation through challenge and support.

The social environment is a prime determinant of overall well-being, according to Erikson. As children move into adolescence, Erikson explained the *identity vs. role confusion* psychosocial stage as a highly influential period of human development in terms of self-discovery. While students are trying to grasp a sense of self and answer the question, "Who am I?" the new environment around them provides a limitless flow of experiences, stimuli, and influences. As they search for the ultimate answer to their question, they must tread through sexual, political, social, career, academic, and many other roles that society deems important. This can result in a great deal of confusion and anxiety for early adolescents.

In relation to identity, Fenzel (1991) examined role strain in the transition to middle school. Students often experience strain in terms of role ambiguity, role conflict, and role overload or underload. The process of discovering "who I am" may be greatly disrupted by the transition into middle school. A student may find it extremely difficult to examine or feel good about his or her capabilities when negotiating a new environment. Similarly, peer comparisons expand exponentially, and inferiority may be an unavoidable aspect of growth. Also unavoidable may be the role confusion that Fenzel (1991) examined in transition. The new middle school student is often assigned new roles to learn (for instance, teams, tracking, homeroom) and may choose others (such as extracurricular activities, new peer groups). As early adolescents struggle to answer the questions surrounding their role in life, they often develop fascinating insights into abstract concepts and alternatives.

The Emergence of Abstract Thought

According to Piaget, adolescence is characterized by a change from concrete operational to formal operational thought. Concrete thinkers (ages 7–11) begin by applying logical operations and principles to explain their experiences and utilize objective and rational thought more than intuition. A typical concrete thinker will subscribe to earthbound, practical applications, often resulting in black-and-white observations and assumptions. As formal thought approaches, these students begin to explore the "gray area" that exists between the black and white, enlightening them to newfound explanations and curiosities. Schave and Schave (1989) considered this "the most drastic and dramatic change in cognition that occurs in anyone's life" (p. 7). Within the social milieu, it is plain to see the differences that exist between early adolescent students with regard to relationships. Concrete thinkers tend to group their peers as friends or enemies. Many middle school students waver hourly, weekly, or daily as to whether they consider someone a best friend or an enemy. As they develop more formal thought, they tend to view their classmates on a continuum, coexisting with varying levels of relationships. They see the gray rather than the black-and-white aspects involved in concrete thinking relationships. To add further to this complexity, variation exists in when and how consistently early adolescents use formal operational thought.

Even so, middle school students tend to question and search for alternatives to new key concepts introduced through school, society, and family. With formal thought tends to come risk taking and rebellious activities on the part of these early adolescents. Although some of these behaviors are cause for alarm for parents and educators, some of this risk taking is needed for students to explore and experience success and failure and to develop their sense of self. For instance, early adolescents who are engaged in formal thinking tend to start questioning school rules and curfews. Similarly, according to Piaget, early adolescents also think about future possibilities, exploring alternatives and options more thoroughly than those who deal only with the "here and now" perspective.

So the transition to middle school brings interesting and, at times, frustrating cognitive possibilities for school personnel. Some students may only be capable of learning and understanding clear new rules and procedures, whereas others may question the size and location of their locker, the amount of time between periods, or why they must dress for physical education class. It may be useful for schools to engage students in more formal operational thought by incorporating participatory activities in orientation programming or team building. For example, including students in classroom rules helps to promote prosocial behavior and formal thinking. This engagement in structured, adult-supervised choices will also help to facilitate early adolescent moral and emotional development.

Moral and Emotional Development

The formation of moral reasoning has been a center of debate for a long time. For instance, Freud's early thoughts on moral development tended to rely mainly on the child's identification with the same-sex parent. Building this relationship resulted in the passing along of values, morals, and standards identified by the child. Once internalized, harsh emotional consequences accompanied any deviation from these values (guilt, shame, etc.). Later, behavior theorists posited that specific rewards and consequences are the driving forces in moral reasoning, and societal norms and conformity to laws dictate judgments. Many believe these theories, focusing solely on behavior and society influence, negated the power of individual thought and intention given to moral thoughts.

Cognitive-development theories much more aptly addressed the view focused on individual judgment and reasoning. Kohlberg suggested that moral development occurs across a series of stages. He suggested that as one matures, the focus on egocentric moral reasoning (preconventional stages) turns toward a more societal view (conventional). Take, for instance, the young sixth grader who avoids bringing his poor report card home to be signed because he wants to avoid being grounded. This child is operating on a self-centered level, making decisions solely to avoid punishment. As early adolescents encounter additional moral dilemmas, they develop into more conventional stages of reasoning, accounting for roles they want to play in society and how well those roles are accepted by others. Students may initiate conversations regarding civil rights, poverty , and other topics that generate conflict between what is "right" and what is "wrong." They may form opinions and base their reactions on what they see as the socially accepted view and stance.

In the transition to middle school, early adolescents are confronted with numerous decision-making opportunities that may raise moral issues and interesting dilemmas. Although culture and a variety of factors also influence moral development, school personnel can create cognitive dissonance (that is, pose a dilemma that cannot be resolved at the current reasoning level), model higher-stage reasoning, and help students navigate decision making to a new level involving respect for others, identification of authority figures, and self-chosen principles. The transition to middle school may include discussions about school rules, cheating, stealing, drug and alcohol use, and a host of other concepts. During the articulation process, students' moral reasoning can and should be challenged to promote more engagement. However, these discussions should be well planned and supervised, as emotional development in early adolescence also influences the transition process.

"Rapid mood fluctuations characterize this period, with the adolescent shifting from intense sadness to anger to excitement to depression in a brief time."[11] Although moodiness, anxiety, depression, embarrassment, and anger are often experienced more frequently, these do occur simultaneously with cognitive, moral, and physical development. A growth spurt that occurs between elementary and middle school will naturally be accompanied by a host of new emotions. Similarly, recognition of changing and more intimate relationships in middle school will be accompanied by judgments (cognitive development) and feelings (emotional development). For example, girls often demonstrate increased depression after the transition to middle school. The major stimulus of moving from elementary to middle school creates a challenge for students to manage and integrate emotions.

Perhaps because of these significant developmental changes, several problematic outcomes are associated with early adolescent development and the transition to middle school, such as declining academic motivation and achievement (for example, decreased feelings of academic competence and heightened anxiety) and increased mental health and problem behaviors (for example, increased depression).[12] Psychological development during early adolescence is characterized by increased desire for autonomy, peer orientation, self-focus and self-consciousness, salience of identity issues, concern for intimate relationships, and capacity for abstract thought.[13] Although the "storm and stress" view remains quite popular, contemporary research has presented a more balanced view of early adolescents.

Contemporary Developmental Research

Although traditional research has primarily described the problems experienced by the developing adolescent, recent research demonstrates that more than half of adolescents do not experience significant problems during puberty.[14] In fact, Roeser, Eccles, and Sameroff (2000) found 40 percent of youth to be well adjusted, compared to 33 percent who had problems based on a variety of academic and mental health factors in middle school for a diverse population. Similarly, several other researchers have indicated that 70 percent to 75 percent of early adolescents negotiate the phase without extreme difficulty.[15] "Adolescence is not a normative time of storm and stress, but many adolescents appear more or less quietly distressed." [16] In fact, most adolescents develop increasing competence and self-esteem over the adolescent decade.[17] Often adults overreact to these overt developmental changes, heightening the conflict.[18]

Eccles et al. (1993) investigated psychological protective and risk factors that are most likely to affect adjustment after the transition to middle school. The increased anxiety and self-consciousness that characterize early adolescent development are negatively related to self-esteem and adjustment after the transition. In contrast, the young person's feelings of competence and personal efficacy buffer the impact; successes in academic and social domains predict self-esteem increases across the transition. For example, Fenzel (1991) demonstrated that personal coping and, in a limited role, social competence mediate the role strain for new middle school students. An evolving body of literature on adolescent coping suggests that students cope in different ways, and their abilities to cope moderate a host of psychological effects, including depression. With the inherent stress in the transition to middle school, promoting coping abilities is essential to promoting positive individual development across the transition.

Though personal change may intensify the stress of the transition to middle school, contemporary research views pubertal changes as an opportunity rather than a crisis. Recognizing, understanding, and promoting early adolescent development in the transition to middle school allows school personnel more precise and developmentally appropriate intervention.

Individual development remains important, but it alone does not provide all of the information necessary to understand students in transition. More recent research suggests the environment or ecology may be as important as individual developmental change.[19] Erikson (1968) suggested that adolescent identity development is the collective responsibility of the adolescent and of parents, teachers, and the larger community. As rising middle school students negotiate the developmental path across the transition, adults in charge of the contexts where they live must pave the way. Eccles and her colleagues (1993), based on Erikson's notions, described this as *person–environment fit*, or the quality of the fit between the developmental needs of adolescents and the nature of the social opportunities afforded them by adults and the environment. Although most researchers in the 1980s focused on developmental changes in transition, more recent studies have examined the impact of contextual factors on students' ability to negotiate transitions.[20] In chapter 3, we take a more detailed look at adolescent development in context and the greater significance of environmental influences.

References

1. Cromwell, 1998.
2. Eccles et al., 1993; Blyth, Simmons, & Carlton-Ford, 1983.
3. Eccles, Lord, & Roeser, 1996, p. 60.
4. Vernon, 1993.
5. Ge et al., 2002.
6. Bell & Bromnick, 2003.
7. Craig et al., 2001.
8. Petersen, Leffert, Graham, Alwin, & Ding, 1997.
9. Koening & Gladstone, 1998.
10. Pruitt, 1998, p. 23.
11. Vernon, 1993, p. 115.
12. Eccles, Lord, & Roeser, 1996.
13. Eccles et al., 1993.
14. Dryfoos, 1990.
15. LeFrancois, 2001.
16. Roeser, Eccles, & Sameroff, 2000, p. 464.
17. O'Malley & Bachman, 1983.
18. Vernon, 1993.

19. Anderson, Jacobs, Schramm, & Spittberger, 2000.
20. Anderson et al., 2000.

3

The Systemic and Ecological Transition in Starting Middle School

Although traditional developmental theory has offered warnings about the tumultuous time of puberty and adolescence, it also highlights this stage as a time of challenge and opportunity. In Chapter 2, we discussed individual development across the transition to middle school. Individual development occurs in context, and the interaction between individual development and the ecology plays an important role in the outcomes of youth development. Bronfenbrenner's (1979) ecological theory of human development stressed the powerful impact of individual development in a changing context. For example, Roeser et al. (2000) discovered that middle school environments that emphasize competition and ability and students' feelings of mistreatment are related to multiple negative outcomes for students. The convergence of adaptation (to the environment) and developmental tasks make the transition to middle school a critical phenomenon with respect to prevention and children's mental health.

This chapter specifically details students' changing relationships with parents and the ecological differences between elementary and middle school. Armed with this information, education professionals can create reforms across the transition to cultivate developmental strengths and assets in students.

Maturing Parent–Child Relationships

Although this book focuses primarily on schools and school personnel, we find it entirely appropriate to stress again the importance of family in the ecological change from elementary to middle school. Traditionally, developmentalists have portrayed family relations in early adolescence as stormy and a normative part of moving toward autonomy and individuation.[1] Early adolescents question parental authority and try to scare parents away with assertive or aggressive attempts at independence. Smetana (1989) found the early adolescent period (grades 5–8) highlights the greatest mismatch between adolescent and parent views on authority. This renegotiation of power within the family reflects the early adolescent's desire for more opportunities for independence and self-control. "One moment the teen loudly proclaims the right to independent decisions; the next [parents] may be presented with a minor problem that the youngster seems incapable of handling independently."[2] For example, multiple risk factors for adolescents increase when families do not solve problems well, are unsupportive, or communicate poorly.[3] Other research has demonstrated that children tend to have a harder time adjusting to school if parental work status changes during the transition to middle school.[4]

Even though increased conflict and decreased closeness occur, these do not often lead to detachment from parents, and parent support remains important to adolescent mental health.[5] Wampler, Munsch, and Adams (2002) discovered that better family functioning and a higher percentage of adults in the support network are correlated with better grades and less depression. Families that are responsive to the changing developmental needs of early adolescents often relate to increased self-esteem and self-reliance, greater satisfaction with school, and positive school adjustment.[6] Parent involvement in the transition process sustains parent involvement in middle school, increases communication with teachers, and improves academic achievement and student retention.[7] Eccles, Lord, Roeser, Barber, and Hernandez Jozefowicz (1997) indicated that developmentally sensitive parenting is a protective factor in the transition to the junior high or middle school.

Intense Peer Relationships

Wiseman (2002) observed that cliques are at their worst in the sixth, seventh, and eighth grades. A common definition of a "clique" in schools is a cohesive group that is banded together by common values. Webster defines a clique as a small group of people who shun outsiders. Specifically, Wiseman describes a clique of middle school girls as a "platoon of soldiers who have banded together to navigate the perils and insecurities of adolescence" (p. 19). Unfortunately, many girls do not make the cut, and they are forced out of the group or become targets of bullying by the group. This compounds the issues of self-esteem and acceptance. However, a new breed of girl also emerges—the "gamma girl"—who is smart, confident, and not concerned with popularity.[8] Many researchers have investigated cliques and female students as a social issue. These highly organized groups maintain a social hierarchy rivaling that of many government institutions.

Wiseman (2002) defined a clique as a group that is formed out of a necessity for social acceptance and protection from rejection and low self-esteem. She divides girls into two groups —"queen bees" and "wannabes"—while others use the terms "alpha girls" and "beta girls." The girls classified as alpha girls or queen bees are the clique leaders; these girls are described as girls whose popularity is based on both fear and control. The queen bee is able to use her good looks, charm, socioeconomic status, money, and force to manipulate other girls and weaken their friendships with others.[9] The beta girl or wannabe will do whatever it takes to impress the alpha girl or the queen bee.[10] Wiseman described other positions in the social hierarchy of the clique: the sidekick, the banker, the floater, the torn bystander, the pleaser/wannabe/messenger, and the target.[11] According to Simmons (2002), a gamma girl is defined by what she does rather than by how popular she is; she is sure of herself, does not care about popularity, loves her parents, and is resilient, often athletic, and independent. This independence and self-assuredness is an outgrowth of having been rejected from a group at an early age.[12]

Tips for Parents:
Helping Young Girls Deal with Cliques

♦ Affirm your daughter.

♦ Realize the situations are serious, important, and difficult to navigate.

♦ Don't tell your daughter what to do; instead, describe the behavior you respect, and help your daughter come up with a plan to combat the problem.[13]

Although parents remain a significant source of support, students depend more on friends in academic and social situations.[14] Communication among peers increases dramatically during early adolescence; students clearly feel the need to relate to one another, exchange advice, and establish social patterns.[15] During this transition, peers increasingly influence developmental trajectories (for instance, peer pressure may increase involvement in problem behavior). In transition, the number of students increases, as does the heterogeneity of the student population in terms of race, ethnicity, and social class.[16] The social network from elementary school is disrupted, and students may find it more difficult to communicate with familiar peers. For example, Berndt, Hawkins, and Jiao (1999) demonstrated that students' perceived social competence declined during the transition to junior high.

This is significant because research has shown that students who feel supported and cared for by other students are more engaged in positive classroom life.[17] Wentzel's (2003) findings demonstrate a connection between sociometric status (that is, peer acceptance or rejection) and adjustment to school. The quality and stability of friendships in elementary school, as well as the influence of friends' development during the start of middle school, may have a significant impact on the adjustment to middle school.[18] For example, supportive friendships are beneficial during times of stress, and students with high-quality and stable friendships seem to thrive after the transition. Also important in the peer network, prosocial behaviors, role taking, and intimacy may prove to help students adjust to new groups of students and new social roles. Most of the peer disruption and salience of peer support may be attributed to changes in school ecology.

School Ecology Changes

Historically, the configurations for most school districts evolved into K–8 and high schools. Around the turn of the century, recognition of the significant change between these two settings led to the creation of the junior high—a miniature version of the high school. Over the last 40 years, the concept of the middle school has evolved and flourished because it seems to better suit the needs of early adolescents. Even with changing configurations, Nottelmann (1987) suggested the transition to middle school in the sixth grade and the transition to junior high in the seventh grade have similar effects. Although middle-grades education itself is designed around developmentally appropriate practices, these are not always implemented fully or successfully. Even when they are, the transition from elementary to middle school is still a vulnerable time for students. The transition often involves a move to a larger, more complex environment, with decreased contact and emotional support between students and teachers.[19]

Contrasting School Days

Consider this contrast in sample school days.

A Day Near the End
of Elementary School

Riley hops on her bus at 8:15 AM along with several of her neighborhood playmates—children she has known for six years. After a short ride, she enters the classroom and greets her only teacher, Ms. Smith. At her desk, which she decorated at the start of the year, Riley gathers her materials for the first lesson. Ms. Smith knows Riley well and quietly prompts her attention with periodic glances.

At lunchtime, Riley walks to the cafeteria with her class and teacher. In the hall, she smiles at the nurse and school counselor, whom she has known for five years. After lunch, she gets to play with all of her friends in fifth grade....

The First Day of Middle School

Dalton trudges to the bus stop, where two high school students also wait in his neighborhood. He boards the bus at 7:00 AM for an hour-long trip—the bus will pick up a full load to drop off at the middle school and the adjacent high school. Dalton sits in the front, near the bus driver, in case the older kids start stuff with him again.

At school, Dalton scuttles to the sixth-grade hall. At his locker, jostled by students he does not know very well, he sorts through gym shoes and notebooks to get the materials he needs for the morning. He heads for his first-period class, only to retreat in embarrassment a few minutes later—today is an "odd" day, not an "even" day.

He hustles past groups of seventh and eighth graders to the right classroom, where the teacher glares at him and writes up a pink tardy slip. All through math class, Dalton worries about phys. ed. class and the eighth graders in the boys' locker room, where he will have to change in front of everyone....

Although these profiles will not fit every student or every elementary and middle school, these two scenarios emphasize the potentially potent ecological differences between settings. Complicated schedules, tracking, electives, more bureaucracy, more departmentalization, more homework, new teachers, more teachers, new and larger peer groups, lockers and late slips, competition and cliques—a myriad of new structures accompany the transition into middle school. Often students move from one primary teacher to a departmental program, a more complex schedule, larger population, more involved rules and procedures, and increased responsibilities.[20] Eccles et al. (1993) suggested that a poor *person–environment fit* exists between individual developmental needs and the practices and ecology of most junior highs or middle schools. Their research indicated that most junior highs do not appropriately match the developmental needs of early adolescents. Various aspects of ecological change and developmental fit are highlighted below.

Physical Environment

The first notable change is the physical size of the building and the number of students. Most middle schools are larger than elementary schools and often house two to three times the number of classrooms. Because elementary or primary students have often been at the same school for five years, the elementary building is familiar and students have utilized many of the classrooms and facilities. Upon entering middle school, students must learn to negotiate a much larger space in a very short time. This creates what Rice (1997) termed *organizational discontinuity*. Fortunately, many middle schools have formed "houses" or wings that accommodate most of the academic curriculum by grade. Even so, new middle school students must make their way to physical education and exploratory classes, to the cafeteria, library, and main office. These journeys are no small feat. Students typically travel unsupervised, among students in upper grades, to locations as scary as the gym locker room or an unsupervised bathroom.

Schedule

One of the first tasks that students struggle to master is moving according to schedule. In primary or elementary schools, most students stay with one instructor in a single classroom for most of the day. When they go to other classrooms, lunch, or recess, students typically travel together under adult supervision. One year later, students may have a block schedule in which classes alternate each day in a mysterious rotation. Their friends from elementary school may not be in any of their classes; in fact, they may not take the same courses at all. In even starker contrast, students now negotiate these transitions on their own. Although this may not seem like a monumental step, it is a novel experience, and one brimming with temptation. No wonder students often report tardy slips as one of their many concerns about moving to middle school.[21]

The transition also seems to increase the use of departmentalization and tracking.[22] In elementary school, most students are mainstreamed in classes, and teachers use differentiation inside the classroom to help all students. Some special classes may exist, but most enrichment activities occur outside the typical schedule. Student self-concepts are especially vulnerable when students move from heterogeneous ability groupings in elementary school to homogenous ability levels in junior high. This emphasis on relative ability and comparative performance may be particularly debilitating for poor minority students, who are more likely to be placed in lower academic tracks.[23]

In middle school, students begin a process of segregation by ability or special needs. This tracking occurs at a time when students are developmentally very concerned about outside appearance and tend to make decisions about identity based on abilities. Furthermore, students who are new to middle school have fewer choices for extracurricular participation. Usually, sports and clubs are reserved for seventh and eighth graders. As sixth-grade students attempt to connect and belong in middle school, their nonacademic options are limited.

Some Significant Problems

Consider some of the problems students have found to be significant in the transition to middle school from elementary school.

♦ Elementary schools tend to be task oriented, whereas middle schools focus on performance.

♦ Student–teacher relationships decline from elementary to middle school.

♦ Instruction shifts from small-group and individual instruction to whole-class instruction in middle school.[24]

Classroom and Curricular Experience

Middle school reform promotes developmentally appropriate learning environments within the school building. Even so, curriculum articulation is a pervasive need. A logical, continuous, and sequential curriculum allows student achievement to prosper.[25] As we have previously discussed, communication between elementary schools and middle school is rare, and many middle school teachers report using the first part of the academic year as a review or "to see where students are." Achievement declines across transition may reflect this lack of continuity in curriculum from elementary to middle school. These declines have also been described as related to the classroom environment.

One of the most popular theories to explain the risk of the transition from elementary to middle school lies in the classroom environment. Research has demonstrated greater teacher control and discipline and fewer opportunities for student decision making, choice, and self-management in junior high compared with elementary school.[26] Wigfield, Eccles, MacIver, Reoman, and Midgely (1991) and others have reported stricter evaluation practices and noted that teachers feel less efficacious in middle school. This has been especially noteworthy in mathematics classrooms.[27] Researchers also note a greater emphasis on social comparison, relative ability, and competition.[28]

These differences between elementary and typical middle school classroom environments have been associated with negative shifts in motivation after the transition.[29] How competent students feel at learning and whether they value what they are asked to learn relate directly to academic and social success and problems during middle school.[30] In fact, a sense of competence and efficacy in the academic domain is the factor most likely to influence whether students earn good grades. Roeser et al. (2000) also demonstrated that student perceptions of emphasis on mastery and effort (rather than ability) and meaningful curricula are related to positive outcomes in middle school students.

Giving more autonomy and recognizing effort are not simple tasks for middle school teachers in today's school environment. The emphasis on accountability and the associated testing regimen pose challenges. Even so, classroom environments can be structured with student participation in mind; student interests can shape curriculum outlines and classroom lessons. This is especially important in achieving an appropriate developmental fit for new middle school students.

Teacher Relationships

Wigfield et al. (1991) and others have reported less personal and positive student–teacher relationships after the transition to middle school. It is becoming more evident that, compared to elementary school, middle school students have less personal connection to teachers. Roeser et al. (2000) found that perceived positive teacher regard and teacher emotional support yield positive outcomes in middle school students. Berndt et al. (1999) also demonstrated that general self-esteem declined in a traditional junior high (with different teachers and classes each period), whereas self-esteem changed little in a junior high organized into teacher teams.

Researchers have highlighted the importance of adult relationships to students' feelings of connectedness to school. The Turning Points reforms for middle school advocate advisory periods, evidently to provide at least one adult with a consistent connection (like that of the singular teacher in ele-

---

Nine Principles for Effective Practice

♦ Believe that every child has the ability to learn.

♦ Seek to make learning an enticing and fundamental experience for both the student and the teacher.

♦ Enhance programs by integrating the curriculum with other subject areas.

♦ Teach the curriculum with an interdisciplinary approach.

♦ Incorporate music to enhance curriculum studies.

♦ Include in every lesson a kinesthetic activity that enhances the quality of learning.

♦ As educators, be prepared to take a risk and play the learner's role from time to time.

♦ As administrators, support teachers by displaying trust. This makes teachers responsible for assessing their own effectiveness.

♦ Establish a community of learners from the start.[31]

---

mentary school).[32] At a time when adult relationships in school seem critical, current research finds them wanting.

In considering motivation, researchers have asked two questions to capture the most important motivational constructs: "Can I succeed on this task?" and "Do I want to succeed on this task?" Constructs relevant to the first question include students' self-concepts of ability, expectancies for success, efficacy beliefs, and perceived control. The second question relates to students' valuing of achievement, goals or purposes for achievement, and anticipated effort.[33] Anderman and Midgley (1996) found that as students moved to middle school, there was an increased focus on ability goals in math and English, rather than the task-oriented focus of the elementary level. This resulted in a significant decrease in academic efficacy across the transition from fifth to sixth grade, with some improvement in seventh grade.

Eccles et al. (1993) determined the quality of the teacher –student relationship is associated with students' academic motivation and attitudes toward school. Students who moved from a supportive elementary teacher to a low supportive teacher in middle school showed a decline in ratings of intrinsic value, perceived usefulness, and value of subject matter. Low-achieving students were particularly at risk for declining motivation when they moved to less facilitative middle school environments. Eccles also suggested that declines in motivation, though often associated with the early adolescent period, arise more from the mismatch between students' needs and the opportunities afforded them in traditional middle schools.

For example, students at the middle school level need autonomy and the ability to maker their own decisions. Researchers in this area indicate that students often do not have these opportunities.[34] Midgley and Feldlaufer (1987) studied student decision making at the transition from sixth grade through ninth grade and found that teachers and students differed in their perceptions about the extent to which students were allowed to make decisions in the classroom. Students actually indicated they had more decision-making ability at the elementary level. Students who perceived their teachers as putting constraints on their preferred level of participation showed the largest and most consistent declines in interest in math between elementary school and seventh grade. If the design of the classroom environment is appropriate for the developmental level of the students, the declines often seen in early adolescents' academic motivation can be avoided.[35] Teachers throughout the middle school years can provide opportunities for every child to experience social and academic success by utilizing classroom strategies that promote social development, as well as those that address individual learning needs.

Creating a Developmentally Appropriate Context

...[T]o the extent that adolescents perceive teachers and school staff as providing them with opportuni-

ties to develop their academic and social competencies, to exercise autonomous control over aspects of their learning, and to feel cared for and
supported during learning, adolescents' perceptions of their academic competence, their valuing
of school, and their emotional well-being should be
enhanced.[36]

Most middle school reform efforts promote many of the
contextual elements highlighted above. In the transition to
middle school, the environment often becomes less supportive of developmental needs; school personnel should look at
changes in school environment through a developmental
lens.[37] School personnel can take advantage of the change of
school environments to bolster many of the aspects researchers find useful to middle school students. Eccles et al. (1993)
found the extent of declines due to the transition varies, de-
pending on what students experience in schools. A host of
studies have highlighted the importance of feeling connected
or valuing school.[38] School personnel can view connectedness
as a primary outcome goal for transition programming. Also,
some studies have highlighted the particular need for identification with teachers and connection to school environment
for poor minority youth.[39]

Some particularly useful research has examined environmental protective factors or aspects that relate to successful
transitions. Gutman and Midgley (2000) examined academic
self-efficacy, perceived teacher support, parental involvement, and feelings of school belonging with a small sample of
poor African American students. They discovered that academic self-efficacy was particularly significant to academic
achievement. Further, students with high levels of parental
involvement and perceived teacher support had higher grade
point averages than peers with high levels of just one or neither of these factors.[40]

Although most efforts by schools target prevention for
small groups of students, intervention and policies less often
address the organization or restructuring of school environments.[41] Asset-building methods delivered to all students
yield greater benefit, but essentially, the more a school imple-

ments the middle school philosophy (such as Turning Points 2000), the more engaged its students will be, and the more positive academic and behavioral outcomes will be produced.[42]

It appears that a balance of preparation and support for ecological changes is most useful in promoting a successful transition.[43] Preparing students for the changing structure, rules, and organization of the middle school and providing information and teacher or staff support at the start of middle school are both important. Ruble and Seidman (1996) found that when "true" middle school pedagogy was practiced, self-esteem did not decline across the transition. Further, Eccles and Midgley (1989) found that many characteristics of the middle school philosophy (for instance, small house programs, team teaching, and advisory sessions) outlined by Turning Points help to facilitate successful student transitions into middle school. "The transition to a facilitative educational environment, even at this vulnerable stage of life, could result in more positive self- and achievement-related beliefs."[44]

Contextual change is also influenced by the feeder structure in the district. For example, a system in which multiple elementary schools feed into one middle school generates greater contextual change (new and unfamiliar peer groups, norms, etc.) than a linear system. In summation, "The relative importance of the environmental context suggests the possibility that educators can do a great deal to facilitate successful school transitions."[45]

Summary

Personal and contextual transformations are significant during the transition. Because of this significance, the transition to middle school has been a frequent and increasing research topic. Chapter 4 highlights these relevant and informative themes in the research for practitioners' use.

References

1. Blos, 1970.
2. Pruitt, 1998, p. 102.
3. Wampler, Fisher, Thomas, & Lyness, 1993.
4. Flanagan & Eccles, 1993.
5. Petersen et al., 1997.
6. Yee & Flannagan, 1985.
7. Mac Iver & Epstein, 1991.
8. Meadows & Carmichael, 2002.
9. Wiseman, 2002.
10. Meadows & Carmichael, 2002; Wiseman, 2002.
11. Wiseman, 2002.
12. Meadows & Carmichael, 2002.
13. Wiseman, 2002.
14. Vernon, 1993.
15. Branwhite, 2000.
16. Roderick, 1993.
17. Wentzel, 2003.
18. Berndt, Hawkins, & Jiao, 1999.
19. Eccles & Midgley, 1989; Simmons & Blyth, 1987.
20. Weldy, 1995.
21. Akos, 2002.
22. Byrk & Thum, 1989.
23. Oakes, 1987.
24. Alspaugh, 1998b; Feldlaufer, Midgley, & Eccles, 1988.
25. Weldy, 1995.
26. Midgley, Feldlaufer, & Eccles, 1989.
27. Wigfield et al., 1991.
28. Eccles & Midgley, 1989; Schumaker, 1998.
29. Anderman, Maehr, & Midgley, 1999.
30. Roeser et al., 2000.
31. McElroy, 2000.

32. Carnegie Council on Adolescent Development, 1989.

33. Eccles et al., 1993.

34. Mullins & Irvin, 2000.

35. Eccles et al., 1993; Mullins & Irvin, 2000.

36. Roeser et al., 2000, p. 458.

37. Roeser et al., 2000.

38. Dryfoos, 1990; Osterman, 2000.

39. Carnegie Council on Adolescent Development, 1995; Ford, 1993.

40. Gutman & Midgley, 2000.

41. Seidman, Aber, & French, 2001.

42. Seidman et al., 2001.

43. Anderson et al., 2000.

44. Carnegie Council on Adolescent Development, 1989.

45. Feldaufer, Midgley, & Eccles, 1988, p. 152.

46. Anderson et al., 2000, p. 336.

4

Important Themes in the Transition into Middle School

Beyond individual and ecological change, both practice and research have demonstrated important themes in the transition to middle school. Recent school reform efforts have highlighted accountability as an important topic for schools. One way to be more accountable and more precise in educational practice and intervention is to rely on the research previously conducted on educational phenomena. The research on the transition from elementary to middle school, although not comprehensive, is extremely diverse in terms of focus and perspective. Because school transitions involve multiple practitioners, an overview of the research on the transition to middle school from a variety of disciplines is an important consideration in understanding student needs and in designing effective interventions.

As early as 1966, researchers began to study what teachers believed to be a loss in academic achievement associated with the transition to junior high school. In a study completed with 489 students during the transition from elementary to middle schools, Finger and Silverman (1966) found a decline in achievement that appeared to be related to academic motivation.[1] Since 1970, research on the transition between elementary school and junior high or middle school has flourished. Simmons, Rosenburg, and Rosenburg (1973), whose initial outcome study alerted school personnel to the risk inherent in the transition from elementary school to junior high, determined that academic achievement and self-esteem decline as students make this transition. Since then, some research has replicated the findings of declines in grades,[2] school satisfaction and motivation,[3] and self-efficacy or self-esteem.[4] The significant risk associated with the transition has led researchers from a variety of fields to examine the effect of the normative transition to middle school.

Perceptions: Student, Parent, and Teacher

Student Perceptions

Because of the academic declines found in the early research, many have illuminated the voices of students who feel intimidated, nervous, or excited about the transition. Students have voiced concerns about navigating the larger building and getting lost, being late to class, being victimized by older students, meeting higher academic expectations, making new friends, and following new rules.[5] Even so, these studies and others have differed as to what types of concerns are most important to students. Diemert (1992) found that social needs (such as making new friends) and procedural needs (such as knowing school rules and the consequences for breaking them), as opposed to academic needs (such as knowing how to get extra help from teachers), were most important for fifth-grade students in a middle school. Arth (1990) revealed seven middle school transition concerns that were acknowledged by 25 percent or more of a sample of 1,068 students in four states. In order of endorsement, they were failure, drugs, giving a presentation in front of classmates, being sent to the principal or assistant principal's office, being picked on, unkind people, and keeping up with assignments. This academic emphasis highlights that students, schools, and perhaps districts may differ significantly in terms of student needs.

In addition to differences in the priority of concern, the studies differ with respect to how difficult students actually perceive these transitions to be. Three studies found that aspects of the middle school transition both attract and challenge students.[6] The attractive features include meeting new peers and enjoying increased freedom,[7] as well as having their own lockers, having different teachers for several subjects, choosing classes, moving to different rooms for various classes, eating in the cafeteria, participating in the sports program, and having the opportunity to make new friends.[8]

Students experience a variety of fears even before they enter the middle school doors. Researchers have found that new middle school students' greatest fear is getting lost, followed by difficulties finding and opening lockers and bringing materials to the right class at the right time. Rising middle school students are also worried about finding bathrooms and getting on the right bus when it is time to go home.[9] Additionally, Akos (2002) discovered that students are concerned about getting bullied by older students and doing well in classes. These concerns are often compounded by the fact that students must adjust to traveling longer distances to school, eating in a larger cafeteria, and changing clothes in a locker room.[10]

Akos (2002) surveyed sixth graders at midyear to determine what they perceived to be the most difficult aspects of middle school. Twenty-six percent of the participants responded with the fear of getting lost and 13 percent responded that making friends was difficult. Other answers included learning the class schedule and getting to class on time. Students also indicated in the survey results those who had helped them the most with the transition to middle school. The top response was friends, followed by teachers and parents.

In terms of adjustment to the new school, Arowosafe and Irvin (1992) found that transition was a persistent theme for their middle school students, and the adjustment phase took as long as half the school year. In England, Brown and R. Armstrong (1982) found that student concerns following a school transition varied by term, with worries about making and keeping friends predominant in the first term and worries about school work and routines salient in the second term. Similarly, Brown and M. P. Armstrong (1986) noted that students' enduring worries following the transition related to class work, homework, and strict teachers. It seems that student concerns vary in both priority and timing.

Student Concerns About School Transition

When questioned about concerns involving school transition, students listed the following areas of concern:

♦ Getting to class on time

♦ Finding lockers

♦ Keeping up with "materials"

♦ Finding bathrooms and lunchrooms

♦ Getting on the right bus

♦ Crowded hallways

♦ Class changes

♦ Personal safety[11]

Parent and Teacher Perceptions

Fewer studies have examined the parent or teacher perceptions involved in school transitions. This is surprising, as studies have found that significant others can both assist and impede the middle/junior high school transition. Arowosafe and Irvin (1992) reported that parents and siblings or peers often communicate warnings or negative or sensationalized information (for instance, tales of fighting or violence) about middle school. In the Akos (2002) study, friends, followed by parents and teachers, were the most helpful to students in navigating the middle school transition.

Concerning parents, Akos and Galassi (2004b) found parents in close agreement with their students about the difficulty level of the transition, the top student transition concern (such as the amount of homework), and the overall difficulty of the transition. Middle school parents and students also agreed about the top positive aspects of the middle school transition for students. Transition programming may have played a role in what parents perceived as students' relatively quick adjustment (one month or less for the majority of students) to the new school in this study.

Unlike students and parents, teachers at the middle school level tended to focus more on the challenges presented by social and procedural rather than academic issues.[12] Teachers also perceived the transition as significantly more difficult than students did. Weldy (1991) highlighted a similar list of challenges that students face in the transition reported by teachers, many that students also mentioned.

Practitioner Implications of Perception Research

The limited research on parent and teacher perceptions and the variance in the research on student concerns make it difficult to highlight precise implications for practitioners. Student, parent, and teacher perceptions most likely vary according to school context of the elementary and middle school, individual student needs, and school programming efforts. Even so,

> students appear to identify three primary categories of school transition concerns—academic, procedural, and social. Academic concerns focus on coping with increased homework and more difficult courses. Procedural concerns involve navigating around and dealing with the complexities of a larger school environment including multiple classes taught by different teachers, while social concerns include fitting in and making new friends, getting along with peers, and coping with bullies or older students.[13]

Needs assessment data can help to inform and prioritize programming efforts. It may be useful to organize transition programming around these core issues and conduct comprehensive needs assessments of students, parents, and teachers about transition needs relevant to individual districts and schools. These data could also be used to set outcome goals that are useful in determining the effectiveness of transition interventions.

Outcomes

In light of today's focus on accountability, outcome studies—more so than perception data—offer insight on the effects of the transition to middle school. The majority of these studies have enumerated negative outcomes associated with the transition. Most often, outcome investigations have demonstrated a significant decline in grades or achievement associated with the transition from elementary to middle school.[14] This includes specific declines in academic self-concept and motivation.[15] Student academic adjustment seems to recover, as declines in achievement typically improve to previous levels near the end of the transition year.[16]

In addition to achievement, research has also demonstrated self-esteem losses associated with the transition from elementary to middle school.[17] These losses, however, may be temporary. Longitudinal research suggests that self-esteem recovers during the transition year.[18] Perhaps related, students' social and athletic self-concepts also decline over the transition year.

Other outcomes have been found in individual studies. Pellegrini and Bartini (2000) demonstrated that students initially decrease contact with peers during the transition, but the quantity of peer relationships recovers quickly. In contrast, they suggest that close relationships decline, more students feel isolated after the transition, and neither of these seems to recover. Seidman, Allen, Aber, Mitchell, and Feinman (1994) also found dramatic changes in peer and school contexts that related to increased daily hassles with school and declines in both social support and extracurricular activity. They suggested these declines are independent of age, grade of transition, or ability level.

It appears evident that, like perception research, outcome research also varies. A few outcome studies have failed to replicate some of the losses found in the research. Even so, the multiple investigations that demonstrate risk associated with the normative transition require attention. Implications for practitioners include the need to examine outcomes in the local context and the need for a more precise understanding of the factors related to declines. To further explore the outcomes, several investigations have looked to individual, school, and peer or family factors for explanations.

Factors Related to School Transitions

Individual Factors

There has been mixed speculation on which students struggle most with school transitions. Early research demonstrated greater self-esteem declines in girls,[19] perhaps a result of the salience of peer networks[20] or the physical impact of puberty in the dual timing of the transition. Research has also demonstrated that girls experience more depression than boys over the elementary to middle school transition.[21] Girls may use different coping strategies and use peers for social support in distinct ways. At the same time, studies have not been able to replicate the gender differences in self-esteem.[22] Further, research has demonstrated more pronounced achievement declines, lower grade point averages (GPA), and a reported lack of assistance with academic needs for males.[23]

In addition to gender, race has been another focus of transition research. Several researchers have suggested that minority status may intensify negative transition outcomes.[24] Seidman et al. (1994) speculated that urban minority students are often located in overcrowded classrooms in larger schools that are entrenched in red tape. They hypothesized that environmental conditions of high poverty and less space intensify the contextual transition and potentially lead to more detrimental effects, such as disproportionally high rates of education failure for urban minority youth.[25]

Gutman and Midgley (2000) also investigated transition effects on African American students and found significant achievement losses from elementary to middle school. Research has suggested that grade declines may be more severe for African American students than for European American students.[26] Simmons, Black, and Zhou (1991) discovered that African American students showed greater decreases in GPA and more dislike for school after the transition from elementary to middle school. In high school, Maute (1991) found that Asian students and students defined as "other" (not White, Black, or Latino) demonstrated more intense high school concerns than other students. They were especially concerned about "being with kids of other races" and "being liked by others." In addition, gender and racial differences in transition concerns varied according to the school attended.[27]

In a more recent study, Wampler, Munch, and Adams (2002) examined racial differences in GPA trajectories during the transition to junior high. They discovered that grade trajectories differed for race but not for gender. Specifically, African American students' GPAs remained "steady" over the transition, Anglo students experienced slight declines, and Latino students faced steep declines, with some rebound effect near the end of the year.

Perhaps intuitively, students with prior academic or behavior problems are likely to have more difficulty with the transition. For example, Anderman (1998) found greater achievement declines in students with learning disabilities. Many of these factors are confounded and do not serve to predict poor negotiation of transition; rather, they may alert school personnel to be proactive in serving the students who may be most in need.

Some exceptions have been reported. Although Gutman and Midgley (2000) found achievement losses for African American students, those who felt more academically efficacious retained higher grade point averages. In another small-scale study, Forgan and Vaughn (2000) found that Hispanic learning-disabled students demonstrated few differences in academic self-concept across the transition. Although these individual factors (gender, race, learning disabilities) are important, research is yet inconclusive, and school personnel may be more influential in manipulating the various systems (school, peers) that also affect transitions.

School Environment

As we have previously discussed in detail, the school environment plays a significant role in the transition. Most of the literature on school context bemoans the poor person–environment fit between most middle schools and early adolescent development.[28] Although the middle school movement has framed reforms to achieve developmentally appropriate environments, many middle schools emphasize competition, tracking, and a controlling environment that may negatively affect a student's transition experience. For example, Anderman, Maehr, and Midgley (1999) demonstrated that students who moved to a school that was primarily task focused (rather than performance focused) exhibited fewer negative shifts in motivation after the transition.

Other examples have also been shown in research. Pelligrini and Bellini (2000) suggested that higher levels of proactive aggression and the endorsement of bullying in the middle school may negatively affect the transition experience. Seidman et al. (1994) suggested that outcomes may depend, in part, on school size and setting (for instance, urban vs. suburban). Districts with multiple feeder schools seem to intensify the declines in achievement.[29]

Queen (2002) stated that school size has a direct negative impact on student achievement and success. Currently, researchers suggest that large schools tend to have low rates of activity, decreases in attendance rates, and increases in dropout rates.[30] Alspaugh (1998a) noted that as school size increases, there appears to be an "associated decline in achievement test scores." School size and socioeconomic status interact to influence student achievement; however, as school size decreases, the effect of socioeconomic status tends to decrease and has a limited effect on student academic achievement.

In response to the constraints of school size, instruction changes from self-contained classroom instruction with the same set of peers to instruction with up to five different teachers.[31] Middle schools are able to combat the negative effects of school size through teaming. In 1994, Waggoner determined that elementary students and middle school students who were involved with teaming performed better academically and felt more connected to the school than students involved in self-contained classrooms. Additionally, elementary students who experienced teaming felt less anxious about the transition to middle school. Teaming increases student involvement and decreases disassociation with the school through smaller, more focused groupings. This implies that "students placed in relatively small cohort groups for long spans of time tend to experience more desirable educational outcomes."[32]

Currently, there is some controversy as to where the sixth grade belongs. Parents tend to feel that students are more successful in the elementary school configuration, whereas educators and researchers state that many sixth graders are ready for middle school.[33] When interviewed, 66 percent of students in the seventh grade said they would have been more prepared for seventh grade and middle school if they had had more than one sixth-grade teacher.[34] The point at which transition occurs also seems to matter with regard to academic achievement. For female students, being older than classmates tends to lessen the stress of transition and hold self-esteem intact. According to Mullins and Irvin (2000), students who transitioned between grades six and seven had the most dramatic drop in grade point average compared to students who transitioned between grades five and six or who remained in a K–8 school. The students who remained in the K–8 school had significantly lower drops in grades than students who attended 6–8 middle schools. Middle school students had a statistically significant deficit in achievement gain compared to students who attended K–8 schools.

The drop in achievement gain and higher dropout rate have prompted many school districts to move from the middle school concept to the K–8 model. For example, the Cincinnati Public Schools moved to this model in response to achievement loss, discipline problems, and attendance issues. According to the director of public affairs, "Our middle schools were not working." Schools that once contained more than 1,000 middle school students have been converted to K–8 schools and only house between 70 and 150 seventh- and eighth-grade students. The school system aims to eventually convert all neighborhood schools to K–12 schools in the near future. The more transitions a student encounters, the more likely that student is to have academic difficulty and to drop out of high school, regardless of the type of transition.[35]

In 1995, Alspaugh and Harting found that regardless of the time of transition, there was a significant achievement loss during the transition from elementary school to middle school, but that achievement scores tended to recover. In 995, Alspaugh and Harting concluded that both K–8 students and middle school students experience achievement loss during the transition to high school; however, middle school students experience a greater loss than K–8 students. The students who experience two or more transitions prior to ninth grade have a greater probability of academic difficulty or quitting high school.[36] Positive relationships between students and teachers, student participation in extracurricular activities, and smaller school size contribute to lower dropout rates.[37] Consequently, school districts may want to reconsider having students experience the school-to-school transitions associated with intermediate-level schools between elementary schools and high schools.[38]

The district and school environment appears to have significant impact on the transition experience. District configurations appear to be based on enrollment figures and economics rather than student transition needs. For example, much research has demonstrated the advantages of smaller learning communities for student achievement, yet large high schools still dominate the landscape of the U.S. educational system. Practitioners can advocate for clear feeder patterns and students moving in intact groups, but they probably can have more influence over their own particular school culture and context. Following the research of Eccles et al. (1993), truly grasping the middle school philosophy may help to promote more successful transitions in the middle school.

Family and Peer Environments

Eccles, Lord, Roeser, Barber, and Hernandez Jozefowicz (1997) indicated that developmentally responsive parenting is a protective factor in the transition. In terms of the family environment, Kurdek, Fine, and Sinclair (1995) discovered that students with moderate levels of family supervision, low levels of autonomy, and high family acceptance and peer norms demonstrated significantly higher achievement across the transition. Wampler et al. (2002) found that students with a higher number of adults giving social support and better family functioning had higher grades during the sixth-grade year. Lord and Eccles (1994) demonstrated that supportive parenting was associated with gains in self-esteem across the transition, whereas Grolnick, Kurowski, Dunlap, and Hevey (2000) found that maternal resources yielded benefits to students' perceived competence, behavior, and motivation. As noted previously, the messages that family and peers provide about the middle school transition are influential.

Even as parents perceive a less welcoming environment in middle school, current research makes it very clear that continued parental involvement is key in the successful transition of students. Participation at this level will foster the likelihood of parental involvement in the high school years. "Parental involvement in young adolescent students' transition from middle school to high school is critical....When parents stay involved in the student's transition...they tend to stay involved in their child's school experience, and when parents are involved in their student's high school experience, students achieve more, are better adjusted, and are less likely to drop out of school."[39]

What the Research Shows

To assist students and increase the likelihood of successful transition, parents of middle school students should take the following steps:

- Become knowledgeable about the needs and concerns of early adolescent youth involved in transition.

- Help their children turn fears about transition into positive action by learning as much as they can about rules and procedures.

- Attend all school-related functions and support the student's needs and efforts to become independent.

- Maintain strong family connections with students, be alert to signs of depression, and seek help for the child if necessary .

- Encourage involvement; the more connected students feel to the school, the more likely they will be to have a successful transition.

- Remain confident and enthusiastic about student success.

- Prepare students for the new environment by attending orientation at the school, locating bus departure times and location, and purchasing all necessary supplies.[40]

There is a bidirectional influence between family interaction and school performance. Researchers have concluded that to improve student achievement and decrease dropout rates, schools must enhance the family's knowledge about transitional activities, as well as the challenges associated with the new curriculum. They should give families the tools and teach them the varying strategies that will strengthen their ability to encourage their child's academic success.[41] Parents should be encouraged to participate in the education of their children; every child should have at least one adult who is committed to his or her education.[42] If a parent is not available or capable of supporting education, then this adult is a teacher or counselor. This fact reaffirms the importance of student–teacher relationships to student academic success, as well as the importance of parental involvement. Parents must be alerted to their importance to their child's success and should feel comfortable coming to school to interact with staff and to assist their child.[43]

Results are again mixed on the influence of the protective nature of support peer structures. Developmentally, peers tend to take on a larger role, but the disruption of the peer network may lessen the potency of peer support. Wentzel (2003) demonstrated that sixth-grade students who are rejected by classmates are at risk for future behavior problems. Although Berndt, Hawkins, and Jiao (1999) did not find a significant effect of peer support, Hirsch and DuBois (1992) found pretransition support to be a significant factor. They suggest that elementary students with high peer support are more likely to maintain satisfactory peer networks and can rely on earlier peer comfort to cope during times of change. Kurita and Janzen (1996) suggested that parents provide the most tangible and emotional support, whereas peers' informational support is the best predictor of social adjustment.

Summary

The implications of outcome research are significant. There is convincing evidence that the normative transition between elementary and middle school has associated risks. Risk has been established most often in terms of academic achievement, self-concept, and self-esteem. It is more difficult to predict which types of students are most vulnerable during the transition. Although not authoritative, the studies suggest that females (self-esteem), males (achievement), minorities (specifically Latino and potentially African Americans), and students with demonstrated academic or behavior problems deserve particular attention during the transition. Peer and family dimensions, though not investigated thoroughly in connectin to transition, most likely influence the process. Perhaps the most influential factor for promoting successful transitions is school context.

Support from Parents, Peers, and Teachers

♦ Students from supportive environments—that is, environments in which parents and children participate together in nonschool activities—experience less academic difficulty as they progress through the transition.

♦ Teachers who are more accessible to students at the next level facilitate successful school transitions. Just making themselves available to the students shows concern and support.

♦ Friends can often help students cope with transition-related concerns.

♦ Students benefit when a transition team (consisting of a counselor, teachers, and students) is in place to help them understand the academic rigor and cocurricular options.

♦ Simply providing students with information about the transition can help them through the transition phase.[44]

As mentioned for both perceptions and outcomes: Schools and school districts should examine the particular effects of their own transition experience. Not all students who struggle in the sixth grade are doing so because of the transition. By examining school database records, schools can pinpoint which students experience declines due to the transition. By looking at patterns of elementary school data (grades, behavior, and attendance) in comparison to middle school data, schools and districts can identify specific positive and negative pathways. School personnel can use this data to single out factors of successful and unsuccessful transitioners to identify risk/asset and protective factors that may relate to increased risk.

Using Thematic Frames
for School Transitions

Research and practice have yielded several useful thematic frames for understanding school transitions. Taken together, many investigations establish themes of academic, personal/social, and organizational/procedural needs that can assist those who seek to intervene in the transition. Others have offered additional theoretical explanations for the transition experience. For example, Fenzel (1991) examined transition effects in terms of role strain. He suggested that students experience role strain in the transition to middle school as they enter new relationships with fellow students, teachers, and parents.

Perhaps the most notable theme is person–environment fit, applied by Eccles and her colleagues. Person–environment fit suggests that individual development interacts with a developmentally appropriate context to either facilitate development or detract from it. For example, consider goal orientation. Many speculate that most elementary schools are more task focused (on mastery, for example), whereas middle schools are performance based (that is, proving competency to others). This may be one area where a developmental mismatch occurs. Fenzel (1991) has written about the role overload or underload experienced by new students in middle school as a result of low perceptions of autonomy, poor developmental fit, or one's own expectations.

Based on person–environment fit, the notion of "anchor points" may be a particularly useful application. Koizumi (2000) suggested that anchor points are useful aspects of the environment that facilitate student adjustment. She noted that school personnel can plant or utilize anchor points—such as information, home-base classrooms, lockers, older siblings, and teacher advisory programs—that help students structure the surrounding environment so that it becomes meaningful to them. These notions of developmental fit contribute to the middle school concept. It may be particularly useful to examine transition years (fifth and sixth grades) in terms of developmental fit and explore how these contexts interact with individual development (as discussed in previous chapters).

Although they are not always presented in terms of school transitions, additional concepts can aid those who work to promote successful transitions. Outcomes may be measured in terms of grades, behavior, and self-esteem, but connectedness to school may offer a better indicator of successful transition. To help guide intervention efforts, school personnel may assess students' connectedness to school after the transition. Emerging research on school engagement is demonstrating behavioral (homework completion and attendance, for example), cognitive, and affective indicators that may be useful for school personnel to monitor.

Another useful theoretical guide in creating programming may be individual assets and asset-enhancing environments (often called protective factors). School personnel may plan transition programs to build the characteristics within students that research suggests promote successful transitions, such as coping abilities, problem solving, and social skills. Orientation programs, school tours, and student ambassadors may be viewed as part of an asset-enhancing environment provided by the school. A family environment that stays engaged in the student's academic work and renegotiates family roles can also promote assets. Similarly, maintaining and building students' peer networks may serve as additional context that supports student transitions.

Although the theory–practice connection is notably weak in many educational endeavors, managing transition programming in the absence of theory is very difficult. The multidimensional nature of the transition and the variety of educators involved require an organizing framework. Although the particular needs and outcomes specific to each school or district are primary concerns, transition programs organized around theory have research backing and offer systemic means of intervention.

Interventions and Programs

Various authors have provided models for transition programming. Many of these are based on theory, outcome, and perception research and offer interesting ways to help students negotiate the transition. Extensive contemporary examples from schools around the country are provided in chapters 5 and 6, and a brief summary of those available in the published research are detailed here. In a national sample of public school students, those who had full transition programs (involving parents, administrators, and students) were less likely to drop out of high school. These students had greater academic success than those who either had partial programs or no transitional program available at all.[45]

Attributes of Successful
Transition Programs

♦ Sensitivity to the anxieties accompanying a move to a new school setting

♦ Awareness of the importance of parents and teachers as partners in this effort

♦ Recognition that becoming comfortable in a new school setting is an ongoing process, not a single event [46]

Anderson et al. (2000) suggested that preparedness (academic and coping mechanisms) and support (home environments, teachers, peers, and information) can combine into a comprehensive program that may help to promote successful adjustment. Akos and Galassi (2004b) suggested tours, scavenger hunts, and practice days as relatively short-term interventions to help negotiate the organizational transition. For the academic transition, study and time-management skills, organizational skills, tutoring, increased communication of expectations (through Web sites and homework hotlines), and vertical teaming may help. For social adjustment, small-group activities, team building, and cooperative learning may increase students' ability to network with peers. Administratively, information exchange and the continuity of curriculum also appear to be important.

Mac Iver and Epstein (1991) also found that an extensive articulation program (using three or more transition activities) increased the likelihood of student success in the first year of school. Even so, surprisingly few published investigations have examined the effectiveness of transition programming. Ferguson and Bulach (1994) investigated the social adjustment levels of fifth-grade students who shadowed sixth graders for one school day. Students who participated in the program scored higher on social adjustment (finding their way around, no problems at lunch, less scared), and teachers felt the program was effective. Although authors have recommended transition groups, coping skills curricula, and other interventions before students make the transition to middle school, these have yet to be strongly established nationally.

Most often, transition programming is offered once students arrive in middle school. Leland-Jones (1998) investigated an eight-month, peer counselor mentoring and tutoring program for students new to middle school. Compared to sixth-grade students the previous year, the intervention year saw a decrease in referrals, absences, and help forms, along with a mild boost in grades and students' ability to articulate and resolve transition issues. Walsh-Bowers (1992) utilized a creative drama group program to promote social skills for students new to middle school. The program led to enhanced social skills and more positive teacher and parent reports. Several others have built transition interventions around coping or problem-solving skills, with moderate success.[47] Using more stringent methodology, Greene and Ollendick (1993) targeted students making a poor academic transition into various group-support interventions. They examined differences between three groups: a control, a group that received additional support from block teachers, and one that received group counseling and increased teacher and parent support. The results demonstrated that that most intensive support yielded improvement in GPA and subsequently had an increased effect.

Although these are useful evaluations, several methodological cautions are in order. The investigations often use self-designed measures, questionable comparison samples, and serve one specific school community. This is significant because few transition programs are stringently evaluated, a small amount of models are available for public consumption, and we have very little evidence on effective ways to promote a successful transition.

Implications

Intervention research may appear most useful to educators who seek established and effective transition programs. Even so, as with perceptions, outcomes, and theory, schools and districts will find it most useful to examine their own particular transition interventions. Because individual and context factors vary, the effectiveness of interventions in school transitions most likely reflects a host of variables. For example, although the previously mentioned interventions provide some data, none of them examine a transition program that extends over the course of the fifth- and sixth-grade years or one that combines multiple interventions. To date, much work remains to be done on understanding the effectiveness of transition programming.

Stetson Middle School, West Chester, PA: A Comprehensive Program

Stetson Middle School's comprehensive transition program is planned and supervised by the building assistant principals.

In April

♦ An assistant principal and guidance counselor visit all feeder elementary schools to meet with their fifth-grade counterparts.

♦ Department chairpersons in English and mathematics visit all feeder schools and meet with fifth-grade teachers to discuss course recommendations and students who will need support in middle school.

♦ Guidance counselors meet with their counterparts at the feeder elementary schools to discuss at-risk students and support structures.

♦ Fifth-grade students discuss their fears and apprehensions about entering middle school in small-group settings with their fifth-grade teachers.

In May

♦ A Stetson Middle School principal, assistant principal, and guidance counselor attend elementary school PTO meetings to introduce themselves to incoming parents.

♦ To facilitate scheduling, a Stetson Middle School assistant principal elicits information from fifth-grade teachers to determine which fifth-grade students should be separated or placed together.

♦ Fifth-grade students participate in letter writing with a sixth-grade homeroom buddy.

♦ A Stetson Middle School assistant principal and guidance counselor visit all feeder elementary schools to meet with fifth-grade students. They provide information about middle school rules and regulations, curriculum, and academic expectations. They also show an orientation video.

♦ Parents are invited to a fifth-grade parent orientation evening, where transition information is presented, teachers and staff introduce themselves, and student council members give guided building tours.

♦ Special education students transitioning to the middle school have IEP meetings at the receiving middle school to revise their specially designed instruction. The elementary special education teacher, a middle school special education teacher, a middle school regular education teacher, and the middle school counselor attend this meeting. A middle school grade-level assistant principal serves as the local educational agency representative at all transition IEP meetings.

In August

Incoming sixth-grade students are invited to participate in a culminating summer activity, Transition Camp, to bring closure to their experience in the transition program and to prepare them for middle school. During the half-day summer camp, students

♦ get to know their principals and some of their teachers.

♦ learn their way around the school.

♦ become familiar with their new rotating schedules.

♦ successfully open a locker.

♦ learn the cafeteria routine.

♦ have an opportunity to meet new friends.

♦ take part in other events to ease the transition.

In late August

Another open house is held for all students new to Stetson Middle School. This "empty schoolhouse" evening allows students and their families to meet staff and wander the building in a less formal setting.

Keys to the success of the transition program at Stetson Middle School are administrators who are committed to making the transition experience a successful one for all students and a highly involved sixth-grade teaching staff.[48]

References

1. Mullins & Irvin, 2000.
2. Petersen & Crockett, 1985; Roderick, 1993; Wampler et al., 2002.
3. Wigfield & Eccles, 1994.
4. Eccles et al., 1987.
5. Akos, 2002; Akos, 2003; Akos & Galassi, 2004b; Lord and Eccles, 1994; Mizelle, 1995; Mizelle & Mullins, 1997; Odegaard & Heath, 1992; Scott, Rock, Pollack, and Ingles, 1995; Weldy, 1991.
6. Akos, 2002; Akos & Galassi, 2004b; Odegaard & Heath, 1992.
7. Akos, 2002; Akos & Galassi, 2004b.
8. Odegaard & Heath, 1992.
9. Akos, 2002; Shumacher, 1998.
10. Elias, 2002.
11. Anderman & Kimweli, 1997; Arowsosafe & Irvin, 1992; Odegaard & Heath, 1992; Weldy, 1991.
12. Akos & Galassi, 2004b.
13. Akos & Galassi, 2004b.
14. Alspaugh, 1998b; Anderman, 1998; Crockett, Petersen, Graber, Schulenberg, & Ebata, 1989; Gutman & Midgley, 2000; Seidman et al., 1994.
15. Eccles & Midgley, 1989; Wigfield et al., 1991.
16. Alspaugh, 1998b; Crockett et al., 1989.
17. Seidman et al., 1994; Blyth, Simmons, & Carlton-Ford, 1983; Wigfield et al., 1991.
18. Jones & Thornberg, 1984; Wigfield et al., 1991.
19. Blyth, Simmons, & Carlton-Ford, 1983; Crockett et al., 1989; Eccles et al., 1993.
20. Mizelle & Mullins, 1997.
21. Blyth, Simmons, & Carlton-Ford, 1983; Hirsch & Rapkin, 1987.

22. Crockett et al., 1994; Seidman et al., 1994; Wampler et al., 2002; Wigfield et al., 1991.

23. Chung, Elias, & Schneider, 1998; Diemert, 1992; Wampler et al., 2002.

24. Cauce, Hannan, & Sargeant, 1992; Mosely & Lex, 1990.

25. Seidman et al., 1994.

26. Simmons et al., 1991.

27. Maute, 1991.

28. Eccles et al., 1993.

29. Alspaugh, 1998b; Anderman, 1998.

30. Alspaugh, 1998b; Pittman & Haughwout, 1987.

31. Ferrandino, 2002.

32. Alspaugh, 1998b, p. 26.

33. Cromwell, 1998.

34. Waggoner, 1994.

35. Alspaugh, 1998b; Crockett et al., 1989; Queen, 2002.

36. Alspaugh, 1998a, 1998b; Newman, Lohman, Newman, Myers, & Smith, 2000; Queen, 2003.

37. Alspaugh, 1998b; Newman et al., 2000.

38. Alspaugh, 1998b.

39. Mizelle & Irvin, 2000.

40. NMSA, 2002a; Robertson, 2001.

41. Newman et al., 2000.

42. Newman et al., 2000; Queen, 2002.

43. Mizelle & Irvin, 2000.

44. Anderson et al., 2000.

45. Smith, J. B., 1997.

46. NMSA, 2002a; Cooke, 1995; Bohan-Baker & Little, 2002.

47. Elias et al., 1986.

48. George Cognato, report to the authors, 2003.

5

Activities and Strategies for Implementing Transition Programs

As we have seen, the school community can do much to ease the transition from the elementary school to the middle school. A smooth transition requires both communication and a strong relationship between the staff of the elementary and middle schools.[1] In this chapter, we highlight activities and strategies that have proved effective at a variety of middle schools.

A Smorgasbord of Strategies

♦ Organize a *Teacher Swap-a-Day:* Middle school teachers teach fifth-grade students and elementary school teachers teach sixth-grade students. This helps teachers from both institutions understand the expectations, routines, and developmental stages of students in various grade levels.[2]

♦ Offer fifth-grade students the chance to *visit and tour* the middle school. These visits include an overview of the middle school structure, brief explanations of academic and extracurricular activities, and a tour of elective classes.

♦ Have sixth-grade guidance counselors lead *guidance sessions for fifth-grade students* during the spring and fall to discuss the middle school curriculum, registration, and scheduling. This is also a good time to discuss expectations and responsibilities. A booklet or pamphlet detailing the information may be helpful at this time.

♦ Hold a *Parent Night* at the middle school to discuss the curriculum, scheduling, and cocurricular activities. Once again, this is a good time to include parents by detailing expectations at the middle school level and the responsibilities of the incoming sixth graders.

♦ Develop a *transition team* composed of elementary and middle school teachers. They should meet monthly to plan and implement transition activities for the school year.

♦ Institute an *advisor/advisee* program in the fifth grade and middle school.

♦ Coordinate ongoing *pen-pal or structured email relationships* between elementary and middle school students.

♦ Develop a program in which students (or even faculty or administrators) can *shadow a student* for a day.

- ◆ Hold *celebrations* that signify the end of the elementary school level and the beginning of the middle school experience.

- ◆ Plan a lively *information fair* to disseminate information related to the middle school curriculum, academics, extracurricular offerings and electives.

- ◆ Offer a *fifth-grade exploratory session* that provides students the opportunity to analyze the connections between academic subjects and careers.

- ◆ Allot time for *middle school students to visit the elementary schools* to discuss the life of middle school students.

- ◆ Encourage sixth-grade subject-area teachers to *review fifth-grade student portfolios.*

- ◆ Arrange for middle school faculty members, counselors, and parents to work together to develop a *five-year plan for fourth graders.*

- ◆ Develop *sixth-grade teams* to aid in the transition.

- ◆ Early in the first semester, *invite parents to evaluate the transition period.* Use the data to make recommended changes.

Other strategies to consider include meetings focusing on course requirements, parent information meetings, individual conferences, mentoring, career counseling, peer mediation groups, and other school presentations. Effective transition programs devised to guide students and parents step by step will ensure the first week of school will be calmer and better organized.

Paving the Way for Transition

The tasks outlined below can frame an effective transitional program that prepares rising sixth graders even before school starts. Many of the activities are adopted from a variety of experts in the field and the research literature.[3] Principals, school counselors, and teachers should choose the suggestions that best fit their school and their students' needs.

Form a Transition Committee

Members should consist of an adequate and diverse representation of fifth- and sixth-grade staff and must share a common philosophy and vision of the transition process. Collaboration across levels ensures an effective transition for all students. One aspect in particular is a mutual understanding of curriculum requirements. Curriculum articulation between school levels is possible only when teachers from both levels are at the table.

Effective Transition Committee

An effective transition committee will

♦ share a common vision;

♦ be committed to serving students;

♦ create a positive school climate;

♦ nurture students' emotional and academic stability;

♦ encourage family partnerships; and

♦ establish high expectations for all students.

Visit the Feeder/Receiving Schools

The transition committee (a group of teachers, counselors, and administrators) should briefly visit the elementary and middle schools for an informal introduction. An awareness of the organization of each school is essential. Activities to consider include the following:

♦ Give a short overview of the school.

♦ Issue an invitation to a parent/student open house at each level.

♦ Briefly introduce fifth- and sixth-grade teachers.

♦ Present a "Day in the Life of a Middle School Student" video.

♦ Distribute passes to future athletic contests and extracurricular events so that students can interact with middle school students.

♦ Pass out handbooks addressing typical first-year concerns and suggesting ways to cope.

Making these contacts at the students' home school enables the transition committee to focus on the new information and may help them to feel more comfortable asking questions.

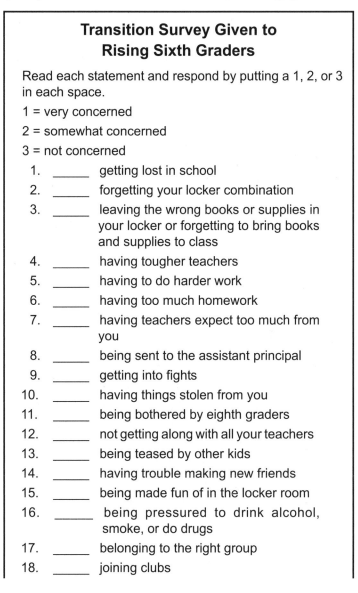

Transition Survey Given to Rising Sixth Graders

Read each statement and respond by putting a 1, 2, or 3 in each space.

1 = very concerned

2 = somewhat concerned

3 = not concerned

1. _____ getting lost in school
2. _____ forgetting your locker combination
3. _____ leaving the wrong books or supplies in your locker or forgetting to bring books and supplies to class
4. _____ having tougher teachers
5. _____ having to do harder work
6. _____ having too much homework
7. _____ having teachers expect too much from you
8. _____ being sent to the assistant principal
9. _____ getting into fights
10. _____ having things stolen from you
11. _____ being bothered by eighth graders
12. _____ not getting along with all your teachers
13. _____ being teased by other kids
14. _____ having trouble making new friends
15. _____ being made fun of in the locker room
16. _____ being pressured to drink alcohol, smoke, or do drugs
17. _____ belonging to the right group
18. _____ joining clubs

19. _____ joining sports
20. _____ liking your teachers
21. _____ new rules and school policies
22. _____ going to the restroom
23. _____ opening your locker
24. _____ finding your way around school
25. _____ earning good grades
26. _____ having enough time to eat breakfast or lunch
27. _____ dressing for PE (gym)
28. _____ taking tests

Host an Open House for Parents and Students

An open house gives students and parents an opportunity to become familiar with daily activities, school programs, staff, and the physical layout of the school.

♦ Share information with parents.

♦ Showcase student work.

♦ Distribute school handbooks on rules, proce-dures, grading, expectations, and discipline policies.

♦ Invite parents to sit down with school counselors to discuss selection of classes and course work.

♦ Give special attention to making every student and parent feel welcome.

One school began its open house with a general meeting in the auditorium, followed by student demonstrations throughout the school building—skits from the drama class, musical en-tertainment from the band and choir, typical math and science lessons, foreign language department activities, and technol-ogy demonstrations.[4]

Five Strategies for Positive Interaction with Parents

Initiate a Dialogue

Instead of leaving parents to form their own views of the school based on piecemeal information, communicate the school's mission and commitments. Invite parents to work with educators to review established programs. Seek to build awareness and support from parents and community members.

Stop Explaining

Parents often perceive a school's attempts to explain its programs as defensive and even confusing. If concerns about program development and effectiveness arise, a committee of parents, teachers, and administrators should hold a meeting to outline both positive and negative aspects of the program in question.

Talk About Academic Achievement

Some parents believe that schools fall short of meeting their children's academic needs. Concerned about the curriculum, teaching methods, and the additional needs of the academically gifted, they expect the school to remedy any problem. A school that acknowledges weaknesses and uses them as opportunities for greater collaboration may boost community and parental support. Invite parents to partner in designing solutions.

Ensure Planned Community Relations

As children grow older, parents find it difficult to stay informed about school events. Establish a liaison team or a transition panel to communicate with parents and community members about student needs. Work with parents to identify information needs and to design communication channels that will provide parents with valid and immediate responses.

Work Toward a Civil Environment

Many parents view middle school discipline as out of control. Behavior that teachers may see as a normal part of

adolescent development may look dangerous and cha-
otic to parents—and to students. Students worry about
gangs, clothing, and profanity and vulgarity in the hallways. To address these concerns, schools should collab-
orate with parents on student behavior standards and
demonstrate to students they are serious about appropriate conduct. Adults should be highly visible during class
rotation, lunch, and other less structured times of the
day.[5]

Establish a Buddy System or Ambassador Program for Students and Parents

Pair each student with a responsible older student and
parents with informative parent volunteers. These buddy systems could provide support and encouragement during the
school year. Hertzog & Morgan (1998) suggested that students experience a greater need for friends during the first
year of transition. Most students will seek companions to sat-
isfy their need to belong. Therefore, it is useful to pair them
with a good role model to lay the foundation for a healthy network of companionships. Similarly, the buddy system for parents fosters a network of parents who support the school's
success. Consider the possibilities:

♦ The school could offer buddy dances, banquets,
and other social gatherings.

♦ Student buddies could begin exchanging letters
right away and continue to do so during the
school year.

Strategies for Encouraging a Collaborative Relationship Between Elementary School and Middle School Children

♦ **Establish a pen-pal program** from the beginning of the year (encourage e-mail). Students may exchange thoughts, questions, and answers about what it is like to be in middle school.

♦ **Plan several field trips to the middle school campus** (special events: plays, concerts, dances, and assemblies).

♦ **Plan independent time for personal journal entries** so students can write about their expectations, apprehensions, concerns, and hopes for entering middle school or reflect on their experiences.

♦ **Pair an elementary student with a middle school student** and arrange meetings, conferences, and excursions for them.

♦ **Schedule a parent–child scavenger hunt** for the elementary students and their parents. Clues might lead to important places on campus: cafeteria, library, office, computer lab, lockers.[6]

Offer a Shadow Day

Encourage each elementary student to experience middle school without his or her parents by accompanying a responsible, experienced student (perhaps the student buddy) for a day. This gives the student an opportunity to observe another student opening and closing lockers, communicating with teachers and students, participating in special programs such as band or chorus, and experiencing the other daily routines of middle school life.

Maintain Contact During the Summer

It would be a good idea for teachers or students to send an introduction letter to the incoming student. This adds another informal contact between teacher and student, paving the way for a positive relationship. Finally, right before the beginning of school, the transition committee should provide an opportunity for students, parents, and teachers to meet at a casual occasion such as a picnic or barbecue. Make sure the selected buddy parents and students are invited to share this special occasion with each other.

A Rite of Passage: Summer Camp for Incoming Middle School Students

Raleigh County, West Virginia

♦ Raleigh County is still on the K–6, 7–9, 10–12 program for schooling; however, the students are transitioning from an elementary school to a junior high school. All students are eligible to attend the camp at no cost, and four sessions are offered.

♦ During the sessions, which are residential and last for five days, students are exposed to a variety of activities to promote social interaction and relationships with peers.

♦ Students are introduced to one another through a variety of games and activities, then assigned to four different groups to work with for the entire week.

♦ Each group has its own cabin for boys and girls, and students are purposefully grouped with students from different schools.

♦ During the week, students attend classes in the mornings. Each class lasts 50 minutes, with a five-minute break between classes. The classes center on student interests. In 1999, for example, the sessions included hemp jewelry making, model rockets, cooperative games, and education about nutrition.

♦ Afternoon activities throughout the week focus on physical activities such as swimming, rafting, and outdoor nature hikes.

♦ Teen mentors serve as camp counselors throughout the week. Each evening, they lead campfire discussion sessions on topics ranging from drug education to violence prevention to bullying prevention tactics.

♦ Parents of students involved in this program are pleased with the range of activities their children participated in during the camp. Parents also reported observed changes in the level of excitement and enthusiasm their children have about going to junior high school and a decreased anxiety in their children with regard to school.

Bingo and Barbecue

One school hosts a barbecue for all new students and their parents the week before school starts.

♦ The evening begins with an orientation for parents in the gym. Parents learn about such things as attendance procedures, phone numbers for staff, recognition activities, and opportunities for parents to participate in school programs.

♦ Meanwhile, the new students are in the cafeteria, where student leaders discuss involvement opportunities for the coming year and answer any questions.

♦ When students and parents are reunited, they fill out special bingo cards. The cards have squares for each important location in the building—library, administrative offices, counselors' offices, restrooms, music rooms, business office, gym, art rooms, and a site where 20 lockers have been set up for practice in opening and closing. At each location, a staff member stamps the appropriate block.

♦ The completed card is the family's ticket to the barbecue, which is served using the school's cafeteria procedure—providing students still another practice opportunity.

> ◆ During and after dinner, tables are set up where parents can sign up to serve on committees and projects that include everything from volunteering in classrooms to fund raising and chaperoning field trips and dances.

Once the School Year Starts

On the first day of school, the transition committee should provide newcomers with guides and maps to help students find their way to classes, the lunchroom, and so on. In addition, parent workshops should be provided during the school year to provide information on understanding early adolescent development and the middle school context. Counselors need to schedule individual and small-group conferences with new students to interact with them, answer questions, and establish a positive relationship. The school should continue to provide school newsletters to parents and students with information on current events, special recognition, and so forth. Conferences or team meetings during the school year offer opportunities to provide relevant information to parents and students.

Student Transition:
A Comprehensive Approach

Parkwood Middle School
Monroe, North Carolina
Mary Ellis, Principal

Mary Ellis felt that her sixth-grade students were not coming into the school prepared to be successful. Together with the Parkwood staff, Mrs. Ellis established a comprehensive approach to assist students with this transition. Parkwood's Bear Care Program takes its name from the school mascot, the bear.

Late in the Spring:
Establish Schedules and Class Teams

The elementary school develops a background sheet for each rising sixth grader.

♦ Parkwood develops schedules based on students' math test scores, with heterogeneous grouping.

♦ Sixth-grade teachers meet with the principal to establish student teams, each with two teachers. Each teacher teaches two subjects, with math and reading taught in 90-minute blocks. The purpose is to ensure that teachers establish relationships with the students and to give the students a sense of belonging in the school. This also ties into Queen's correlate number, which states that every child must have at least one adult who has a vested interest in the child's educational success.[7]

During the Summer:
Orientation Sessions for Parents and Students

♦ Over two and a half days, small groups of parents and students are introduced to the middle school.

♦ Students and parents meet the principal, guidance staff, and teachers in one general session, then split for individual sessions.

♦ In the student session, the students are given their schedules, assigned their lockers and combination locks, encouraged to ask questions about any concerns they may have, and introduced to skills to assist them with organization.

♦ Students also experience team-building activities and are oriented to the school's physical campus.

♦ Meanwhile, parents are oriented to the North Carolina Standard Course of Study, to the stages of child development and the changes they will experience with their child during the middle school years, to the rules and regulations of the building, and to the campus facilities.

At the Start of the School Year: A Welcoming Aloha Dance

♦ Parents, students, and staff are all invited to this kickoff event.

♦ Parents can meet teachers and staff, students can meet teachers and staff, and rising eighth-grade students are invited to give students an opportunity to meet some of their future classmates. This helps to establish a sense of belonging in the kids as well as a feeling of welcome for all new students and parents.

♦ According to Mrs. Ellis, 88 percent of new students and parents attend the orientation sessions and dance.

Throughout the Year: Monitoring and Mentoring

♦ The Bear Care Program does not end when the school year starts. Students with low test scores are identified, monitored, and mentored by guidance counselors throughout the school year to ensure a smooth adjustment and academic success.

♦ Student interest clubs at Parkwood provide mentoring and establish involvement in the school. The many different clubs include fishing, scrapbooking, even a step team.

Results

♦ The Bear Care Program has led to fewer schedule changes, fewer first-day absences, and few lost students.

♦ The first day of school is much more comfortable for students and parents, and the students report feeling as though the school really cares about them and is excited they are becoming a part of the school family.

♦ The parents praise the program, as do the members of the school staff.

♦ The educators in this school address the needs of students as they enter middle school as well as the issues relevant to a smooth transition.

Other Suggestions

Middle school programs that foster the social, emotional, academic, and physical development of early adolescents include interdisciplinary teams, advisory teams, and a school-within-a-school philosophy. In the interdisciplinary team method, a certain group of teachers works with the same group of students. This fosters interaction among the team members, provides a common planning time, and facilitates shared parent conferences. The programs described in the following pages demonstrate a variety of activities and plans that are effective in each individual school. School leaders should evaluate the following programs and implement components that will be most effective in their schools.

In advisory teams, students meet on a regular basis to discuss concerns and share relevant information. Their advisors conduct activities that foster student motivation, self-esteem, and autonomy, create bonds among peers, or explore career goals. This time could also be used to address individual concerns, such as family problems or health issues. Schools may take advantage of the advisory team and advisory period to foster the transition philosophy and goals throughout the school year.

Middle school teachers need to provide a myriad of instructional strategies to reach all students. Block scheduling that offers 90-minute classes may be more conducive to effective strategies that foster problem solving, develop higher-order thinking skills, and encourage self-learning. Numerous studies suggest teachers need to lecture less and give greater emphasis to student participation—cooperative learning, real-life projects, and project-based learning. These types of instruction enhance critical thinking and problem-solving skills.

Transition Program Ideas, Month by Month

Month	Strategies
August	◆ Invite all new students and families for a self-guided tour. ◆ Hold orientation picnic (eat, practice opening lockers, address concerns). ◆ Mail home student schedules with welcome letter, handbook, supply lists, FAQ sheet.
First two weeks of school	◆ Station student leaders in hallways to assist with lockers, schedules, questions. ◆ Dismiss new students five minutes early to find bus. ◆ Hold an open house for each grade level. ◆ Distribute an activity booklet to all students outlining after-school activities and meeting days.
September	◆ Start transition planning by preparing timeline.
October	◆ Release sixth- or seventh-grade teachers to spend part of the day in elementary school (continue in November).
November	◆ Send letter to elementary principal outlining orientation program. ◆ Send letter to elementary teachers outlining orientation event details.

January	♦ Start sending PTA newsletter to fifth-grade parents in feeder schools. ♦ Invite middle school students to apply to be peer assistants for orientation. ♦ Solidify master schedule for incoming students' orientation visits to school.
February	♦ Mail invitation to Parent Night to incoming students and their parents.
March	♦ Guidance counselor visits each elementary school to outline enrollment procedures and to distribute registration booklets. ♦ AP and special education coordinators visit each elementary school. (District provides substitutes so that coordinators can meet with each fifth-grade teacher.) ♦ "Principal's Coffee" sessions begin. ♦ Fifth-grade teachers spend part of a day in middle school. ♦ Host parent orientation night at middle school. ♦ Implement a program for fifth- and sixth-grade teachers. ♦ Hold follow-up visits with sixth graders, who fill out transition surveys.
April	♦ Host fifth-grade orientation at middle school.
May	♦ Host fifth-grade Parent Night (special programs, handbooks available, tours). ♦ Middle school principal visits elementary classrooms with sixth- or seventh-grade helpers.
June	♦ Invite rising sixth graders to visit for building tour (with seventh- or eighth-grade tour guides). ♦ Offer presentations by coaches and student leadership teams. ♦ Distribute welcome letter and supply list in fifth-grade report cards.[8]

Easing the Transition: Articulation Teams

Lemmel Middle School
Baltimore, Maryland

At Lemmel Middle School, articulation teams ease the transition from elementary school to sixth grade.

♦ An articulation team consists of the sixth-grade administrator, four teachers, a special educator, a parent, and the school principal. The team develops activities that help students from 25 feeder schools transition to middle school.

♦ Transition activities are led by the sixth-grade guidance counselor and student ambassadors (representing all of the feeder schools).

♦ The team visits each feeder school and provides a slide show along with a copy of the Lemmel Orientation Handbook.

In Late Spring: Feeder Schools Visit

Each feeder school visits Lemmel Middle School for an informational program and a tour of the facility. Parents of fifth graders are encouraged to attend.

In Late August: Orientation

Before the start of school, sixth graders participate in a special orientation program. After a welcome from the principal, roll is called and students and parents leave with an assigned homeroom teacher. Students and parents follow an abbreviated schedule of a school day while becoming familiar with the facility, teachers, expectations and rules of middle school, and the necessary supplies.

Staggered School Opening

The first two days of school are only for sixth graders. The seventh and eighth graders begin on the third day.

During the First Month: More Orientation

The school counselor holds a one-hour group guidance session with each sixth-grade class. The counselor explains how to make an appointment for counseling sessions and where the guidance offices are located. In addition, the school counselor introduces students to the Student of the Month Program and the Lemmel Middle School Honors Program.

The librarian also holds an orientation session. The librarian introduces students to the library's different resources, attempts to stimulate students to read for pleasure, and encourages students to volunteer in the library.

Engaging Parents Throughout the Process

In May, before students leave elementary school, parents attend a meeting that focuses on common middle school issues:

- Differences in elementary and middle schools
- Personal responsibility and independence
- Increased number of teachers and subjects
- Riding the bus
- Peer relationships
- The availability of school counseling services
- Ways for parents to be involved in the middle school

During this informative meeting, parents receive a copy of the student and parent handbook for Lemmel Middle School. While reviewing the handbook, teachers explain students' academic responsibilities and other expectations for rising sixth graders. The evening concludes with a tour of the building.

Keys to the Effectiveness of the Articulation Program

- Frequent communication and collaboration among Lemmel Middle School and all its feeder schools
- Sharing of comprehensive information about student behavior, academic achievement level, and special needs[9]

An Abundance of Information— Detailed Timeline

Holman Middle School
St. Ann, Missouri

Students and parents of Holman Middle School receive an abundance of information about the school, programs, the faculty and staff members, the administration, and the school's expectations before entering the doors. The transitional program follows a detailed timeline.[10]

♦ **January: PTA Newsletter** Parents of fifth-grade students who will feed into the middle school begin to receive the school's PTA newsletter. The newsletter provides descriptions of how parents affect the school and suggests ways for parents to volunteer.

♦ **March: Morning Coffee** The principal hosts a session for parents to discuss issues and answer questions about the middle school education level.

♦ **April: Orientation** Fifth-grade students participate in an orientation at the middle school. Students are formally greeted by staff, tour the facility, and view a video prepared by students describing middle school. Afterward, students are provided refreshments prepared by the middle school PTA.

♦ **May: Fifth-grade Parent Orientation Night** School staff and parents of students currently attending the middle school host the orientation. The forum provides parents with practical information about middle school and the programs offered to students at this level. The night concludes with a guided tour of the sixth-grade facility.

♦ **June: Supply List and Welcome** Students receive a supply list and a note from the sixth-grade staff welcoming the rising sixth graders to middle school.

♦ **Early August: Information Handbook** An information handbook is mailed with student schedules and answers to commonly asked questions.

♦ **August: Pre-opening Visit for Students and Parents** The pre-opening visit gives students the opportunity to locate the entrance to the sixth-grade facility from the bus loop, walk through their individual schedules, and meet staff who work closely with sixth-grade students.

♦ **The First Few weeks of School: Orientation** Sixth graders engage in an orientation program that familiarizes students with the facility, the staff, student recognition programs, and the behavior guidelines and expectations for the school community. The school provides each student with

• an assignment planner;

• a school calendar noting important dates and other information; and

• an activity booklet that identifies after-school activities available and the scheduled meeting dates.

Transitional activities continue throughout the first year. The principal and staff at Holman Middle School focus on student success. Parents and students are fully aware of the expectations of Holman Middle School, and students are encouraged to succeed academically and socially.

Fledgling Redhawk Program

At a middle school in southwestern North Carolina, the Fledgling Redhawk program is in place. This program is a combination of many of the other programs described in this chapter. In November, the school holds a meeting for all of the feeder schools' fifth-grade teachers. This gives the teachers from the feeder schools and the sixth-grade teachers an opportunity to meet and discuss issues such as vertical teaming and transition.

In February, the group gets together again and reviews the proposed plan that has been developed based on the input of sixth-grade teachers and fifth-grade teachers from the feeder schools. The program consists of a series of events, all of which culminate with a half-day event on a Saturday in

June. Students from the elementary schools visit the middle schools during late May while the current sixth-grade students are participating in field day, allowing the students from the feeder schools to experience the classrooms and hallways without any other students in them. Prior to this visitation, the administrator who will be working with the future sixth graders conducts visits to each of the feeder schools. Accompanying this administrator on these visits is the guidance counselor, who will work with the students the following year, and a few current sixth-grade students. The administrator also brings a PowerPoint slide show that chronicles a typical day in the life of middle school students. The administrator and team members spend the morning at the elementary school and eat lunch with the students, further building familiarity with some of the middle school staff.

In April, the student information sheet is disseminated to the elementary schools and then collected in mid-May so that schedules can be created. All scheduling is completed by the end of May. When the students visit the middle school during May, there are already familiar faces in place to greet them, and the students feel more comfortable. Each feeder school visits the middle school separately, further facilitating the feelings of comfort in the students. During this meeting, students are able to meet the principal and teachers, find out a little bit about the school and what middle school is like, and tour the school. The visitation concludes with a reception in the cafeteria, where the students are able to mix with selected sixth- and seventh-grade students and get to know some of the teachers. Later that evening, the parents and students are invited back to the school to enjoy a similar program that helps to introduce the parents to the middle school, the middle school concept, and to the actual school building and the staff.

In June, the students and parents are invited back for a day of orientation. This is called the Fledgling Redhawk program (named after the school's mascot), and it lasts from about 8:00 AM until 2:00 PM on a Saturday. During this program, students are able to get their schedules, meet their teachers, find out the expectations of the school and their individual teachers, get supply lists, learn how to work a lock, and meet their future classmates. The sessions are lead by guidance counselors and principals; however, the sessions also include student presentations and a question-and-answer session to gain an accurate student perspective. Not only are students who have enjoyed great successes included in the presentations, but also students who may have had initial academic, social, or behavioral issues are given an opportunity to speak. This is a perspective that is often not seen and proves to be invaluable to students and parents.

The parents are also invited to this session and are able to do all of the above, as well as participate in a question-and-answer session with the principal. Parents are also given an opportunity to tour the building. The culmination of the orientation process is a picnic lunch served on that afternoon. The administration cooks the food, the clubs and the PTO are all present to welcome students and parents into the middle school family. Counselors are available, as are the bus drivers, to answer any questions that parents or students may have. This activity helps to bring the students and their parents into the school community. At the beginning of the school year, the students are far more acclimated to the building, their teachers, and the expectations of the school, thus providing a much smoother transition.

The process does not end with the beginning of school: Students who are having academic or behavioral difficulties during the first weeks of school are targeted by the counselors and receive additional support and coping techniques as the year progresses. New sixth graders also participate in an advisory program to further facilitate the development of relationships with teachers and to remain proactive toward problems, academic as well as social and behavioral, faced throughout the course of the year.

This program is well balanced, staff created, and research based. The students, parents and staff all have a greater sense of comfort and preparedness at the beginning of the year, leading to higher levels of student and teacher success.

Sixth-Grade Orientation

Student Session

8:30 AM—Arrival of students, assembly in gymnasium

8:35 AM—Begin program, opening remarks (principal)

8:40 AM—Introduction of administration

8:45 AM—Transitional issues (administration, done by teams)

+ Lockers/locks
+ Building/lunch
+ Expectations
+ Social aspect of middle school
+ Uniforms

9:10 AM—Students speak

10:00 AM—Dismissal; reception in cafeteria with cookies and juice, student council representatives, student models available at each table

Parent and Student Session

6:00 PM—Refreshments: hot dog supper

6:15 PM—Welcome, introduction

6:20 PM—Transitional issues

+ Rules
+ Expectations—NCSCOS
+ Teachers
+ Counselors
+ Tour of building
+ Locks/lockers
+ Uniforms
+ Programs: Redhawk rewards, conflict resolution, Saturday school, Peach Program, remediation, tutoring (after and during the school day)

Introducing Model Power for Achievement With Constructed Transitions

By April (required)

♦ Set up school and classroom visits for elementary school students. Transition team members, administrators, and selected students should distribute information about the middle school, academic programs, and extracurricular activities offered at the middle school.

♦ Develop a brochure or student handbook to be distributed at visitation that contains school information about the academic demands of middle school, graduation requirements, health records forms, a list of important test dates, information on different programs, clubs academies, and extracurricular activities.

♦ Assign rising seventh-grade mentors to groups of four to six rising sixth graders and develop a way for students to receive credit as part of a service learning project. Develop dates and programs for "meet the faculty" nights in late May and early August.

♦ Develop a survey for incoming sixth graders to collect data about their initial perceptions of middle school. Repeat a second and third survey in six-week intervals.

Highly Recommended

♦ Develop a school-within-a-school Sixth Grade Academy.

♦ Involve current fifth-grade administrators and faculty in vertical teaming. Many schools develop a team or committee to focus on this important activity.

Student Mentors Assisting New Sixth Graders with the Transition to Middle School

Learning for Living, Inc.

The philosophy behind WEB is that students can guide other students to be more successful. The goal of the program is to help students to develop relationships with one another and to learn that the people in the school really do care about them.

♦ The year begins with an interactive orientation session in small groups, led by the WEB leader. Through these activities, students learn about one another, learn about the school campus, and discuss issues pertinent to their success in middle school. The leaders seek to instill a feeling of welcome and excitement in the rising middle school students.

♦ Throughout the course of the school year, the WEB student leaders conduct classes geared at addressing social as well as academic issues, helping to strengthen the bond between the students and the leader.

♦ The WEB program also provides structures for tutoring, recognition of student achievement, and peer counseling.

References

1. McElroy, 2000.

2. Hertzog & Morgan, 1998.

3. Hertzog & Morgan, 1998; Mizelle, 1999; Shoffner & Williamson, 2000.

4. Shoffner & Williamson, 2000.

5. Williamson & Johnston, 1999.

6. Schumacher, 1998, p. 3.

7. Queen, 2002.

8. Pohl, 1991; Combs & Jurgen, 1993.

9. Cooke, 1995, pp. 9–11.
10. Pohl, 1991, pp. 28–29.

6

How Educators Can Ease the Transition

In 1999, Michael Mazarr stated that we are living amid rapid change, traveling swiftly out of the industrial era and into the era of knowledge. The focus is shifting from the building of things to the manipulation of information, emphasizing process over product and valuing relationships over differences. Mazarr described education in today's world as a lifelong process rather than a one-time event. Educators take on new roles and new goals. Rather than preparing students for specific jobs or careers, they seek to develop lifelong learners who will be adaptable to a rapidly transforming workplace.

Education policy at the federal level reflects the impact of the knowledge era by raising learning standards for all children and by supporting efforts to improve schools that serve minority and impoverished children. Former secretary of education Rod Paige intended to spread a culture of accountability throughout the Department of Education.[1] As state governors feel increasing pressure to answer for the level of academic performance among their states' schools, they are demanding more power over school districts. The number of governors who name their state school superintendents and state board members is on the rise, as is their control over education monies.

Ironically, although the bureaucracy appears to be tightening at the top, the trend at the local level is to empower front-line workers in the decision-making process. With the implementation of high-stakes testing and a rising dropout rate, educators face a dilemma: Should they focus their efforts on passing the test or on providing meaningful student learning experiences? Wagner and VanderArk (2001) believed that rebuilding an accountability system that measures the production of quality student work addresses both accountability and the demands of the knowledge era. Presently, a blurring of the boundaries in professional roles at the school site is evolving in response to accountability mandates at local, state, and national levels.

Against this backdrop, this chapter outlines what educators at all levels can do to ease the transition from elementary school to middle school.

The Role of the Central Office

The central office staff, as Robert Johnston (2001) reported, is one of the most underutilized resources available in local school efforts to improve student achievement. Central office staff and their connection to raising student achievement has recently become a topic of discussion and research in school administration preparation programs. Although principals certainly should possess at least one area of instructional expertise, they cannot be experts in all areas. Central office staff can provide the missing knowledge and skills at the school sites. They also should be astute at aligning the budget to address the needs of the instructional program. In addition, the instructional program should be driven by data disaggregations. Finally, school districts should behave more aggressively in "growing their own" effective leaders by providing leadership training opportunities for promising employees. At present, a model school district does not exist. Although some districts contain some high-performing schools, no dis-

Roles of Educators in Transitioning Students from Elementary to Middle School

County Office Staff	School Administration	School Counselor	Classroom Teachers
Provide an overview of transitional programs, designing a general format for the school district to follow.	Set the success of all sixth-grade students as a top priority for the school.	Lead or advocate for transition discussion groups that include orientation, team building, tutoring or mentoring programs, and advisor programs.	Build a team atmosphere among the sixth-grade teachers in relation to behavior, academics, and extracurricular events.
Coordinate plans and mediate issues between the feeder school and the receiving school.	Make scheduling and facility decisions with the needs of sixth graders in mind.	Work with elementary and middle school counselors to create transition groups for rising sixth-grade students.	Cultivate appropriate personal relationships with students.
Provide support through training, materials and time.	Select and motivate quality teachers to teach the sixth-grade classes.	Engage parents in the process of entering middle school.	Be proactive in establishing supportive parental relationships.

County Office Staff	School Administration	School Counselor	Classroom Teachers
	Provide staff development opportunities based on the needs of the sixth-grade teachers.		Communicate with both the elementary school and middle school teachers to create a seamless transition from elementary school to middle school.
	Investigate alternative behavior management plans that meet the needs of the sixth-grade students.		Seek the assistance of support personnel when a student does not appear to be handling transition successfully.
	Actively participate in the county transitional program, working closely with the administration at the feeder/receiving school.		
	Involve parents in the transition phase early.		

tricts possess a consistently high level of performance across all schools.[2] The answer to this inconsistency may lie with the local school-level administrator.

The Role of the School Principal

The principal is one of the most important individuals during the transition period at the school. In addition to handling everyday situations, the principal must establish guidelines to make the transition easier—and then make sure those guidelines are followed. He or she must get the staff and teachers to believe and then empower them to assist in a smooth transition period. As the leader at the school, the principal needs to be proactive in advocating changes that will ensure an easier transition for students. The principal should delegate responsibilities to other staff members who will play a role during the transition process. To underpin the transition program, the middle school principal should establish and maintain a working relationship with the elementary school principal. Together, both principals should hold information sessions concerning the higher level of learning and curriculum articulation across levels. During the sessions, they should make it a point to address parental issues concerning the transition process. It is important at this time to include staff members and invite their input into the discussions. The school may develop a committee that will set up workshops to inform parents about the transition period.

Alternative training programs that are being implemented across the nation reflect the shifting role of the school principal. Preparation for school administration has centered on structured internship experiences, in which interns develop reflective practices and a commitment to transforming schools. "As new accountability measures take effect, a broad consensus that has emerged in education policy circles that raising the quality of school leadership is essential."[3] Thus, the accountability mantra is reshaping the 1980s concept of the instructional leader. "Principals, instead of being building managers, should become leaders of instruction—dynamic, inspirational educators focused almost exclusively on raising student achievement."[4] Part of being a strong instructional leader is the ability to lead staff, students, and parents through a smooth transition.

What exactly does instructional leadership look like? An instructional leader may be an individual who spends a large amount of time in the classroom with the students and teachers. She or he may coordinate instructional materials, time, and staff to support instructional goals. An instructional leader should be the motivating force within a school building and should know what it takes to improve student achievement. However, in addition to student achievement, a principal is also accountable for running the buses, feeding the children, and maintaining a safe and orderly environment. Can one individual perform all of these responsibilities alone? Principals must possess leadership and content knowledge and practice distributed leadership.

Classroom teachers possess knowledge about their content area in great depth. A school administrator will also own that depth of knowledge in a particular area. The principal will also gain a working knowledge of other core academic areas through observation and study in order to discuss and guide all teachers in instructional growth. An effective administrator will build leadership capacity among the faculty based on the strengths of individuals. Ultimately, the role of the principal as instructional leader is to nurture the leadership abilities of classroom teachers as a means of improving instruction and raising student achievement. In a study of recent principal graduates, Burnham (2001) found the training the principals had received in university preparatory programs was more focused on instructional leadership. Queen, Allen, and Burnham (2002) built the case that universities must prepare their principal graduates to be leaders of student achievement.

Classroom Teachers as Instructional Leaders

In "New Roles Tap Expertise of Teachers," Jeff Archer identifies four types of instructional teacher-leaders: the staff development teacher, the lead teacher, the peer assistance and review teacher, and the consulting teacher. Each type of teacher-leader is empowered to assist in improving classroom instruction in specific ways.

♦ The *staff development teacher* works with colleagues to identify instructional areas that need improvement and to design staff development opportunities to address those needs. This person visits classrooms and works in a coaching manner to facilitate quality instruction; however, the staff development teacher does not report observational data about particular teachers' abilities to the administration. The staff development teacher works to improve staff development throughout the school.

♦ The *lead teacher* functions in more of an administrative capacity—for instance, assisting in the hiring of new teachers.

♦ The *peer assistance and review teacher* is "empowered to police" the teachers, providing recommendations as to who keeps their jobs and who does not.

♦ The *consulting teacher* leaves the classroom to help other teachers be successful. This teacher-leader also participates in the evaluation process of their colleagues. After three years, the consulting teacher returns to the classroom.

The success of these positions relies heavily on the principal's ability to select and train the appropriate teachers to serve in leadership capacities and on the professionalism and commitment of the staff.[5]

The school administrator bears responsibility for developing a transition program that fits the specific needs of that administrator's students, school, and community. Careful planning, communication, and implementation will help to provide students with successful experiences and promote achievement at each educational level.

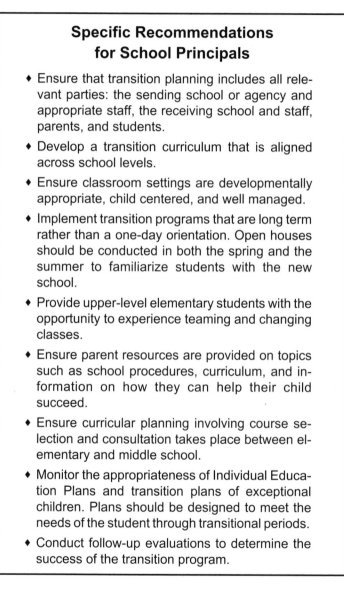

Specific Recommendations for School Principals

♦ Ensure that transition planning includes all relevant parties: the sending school or agency and appropriate staff, the receiving school and staff, parents, and students.

♦ Develop a transition curriculum that is aligned across school levels.

♦ Ensure classroom settings are developmentally appropriate, child centered, and well managed.

♦ Implement transition programs that are long term rather than a one-day orientation. Open houses should be conducted in both the spring and the summer to familiarize students with the new school.

♦ Provide upper-level elementary students with the opportunity to experience teaming and changing classes.

♦ Ensure parent resources are provided on topics such as school procedures, curriculum, and information on how they can help their child succeed.

♦ Ensure curricular planning involving course selection and consultation takes place between elementary and middle school.

♦ Monitor the appropriateness of Individual Education Plans and transition plans of exceptional children. Plans should be designed to meet the needs of the student through transitional periods.

♦ Conduct follow-up evaluations to determine the success of the transition program.

The Role of the School Counselor

For school counselors, perhaps the most common procedure for the transition deals with scheduling. Even with technology, this is an extensive and laborious task. The scheduling process has significant impact because counselors often decide the composition of teams, distribution of special needs students, and placement in ability levels of curriculum. Counselors often work with students who have school phobia or adjustment problems. Because school counselors are embedded in the transition process and because these events shape developmental paths, it is important that school counselors lead transition efforts. Leading transition programs also align with the new American School Counselor Association model, which stresses leadership and advocacy.[6]

The developmental changes and challenges in early adolescence provide a unique opportunity for group counseling because most students report seeking help with the transition from peers.[7] As students begin middle school, peers take on a more important role in the student's life. Both the importance and intimacy of peers increase as students begin to establish an identity outside of the family.[8] In fact, Petersen, Leffert, Graham, Alwin, and Ding (1997) suggested that peer support can be a protective factor for early adolescents and can act as a buffer against negative influences.

Preparing to start a transition group can be one of the most challenging feats to overcome. The following table outlines the major steps a counselor needs to take to have a successful transition program.

Five Steps of a Successful Transition Program

Session	Focus	Activity
1. Introduction and pen-pal activity	Introduction of members, setting of rules, establishment of expectations, and orientation to the group format	May include e-mails, phone calls, or letters to teachers and staff at the middle school. Students could also write questions that are answered by current middle school students.
2. The academic transition	The academic changes that will occur in middle school	Engage students in discussion about managing multiple teacher relationships, multiple teacher expectations, learning styles, test taking, tracking, and collaborative learning.
3. Organizational transition	Rules, expectations, and procedures	Complete missions within the group with a four-minute time requirement. Also provide maps of the middle school to orient the students with major locations. Include in the discussion teacher expectations for homework and classroom behavior.
4. Personal and social transition	Personal growth, development, and social relationships.	Provide opportunities for students to talk with peers about physical changes they may be experiencing. Also prompt students to discuss peer and family relationships.
5. Summary and termination	Establish an identity and what was gained through group process	Have students forecast and provide projections about the transition and have students envision what they will be like in middle school.[9]

TRANSITION 2

Specific Recommendations for School Counselors

♦ Create transition teams in the school. These teams should include teachers, administrators, special needs instructors, parents of students in transition, and even students from transition-year grades.

♦ Define the needs of the students, parents, and school staff.

♦ Prepare and document a yearlong transition plan. This should begin in January of the fifth- or eighth-grade year and end in December of the sixth or ninth-grade year.

♦ Facilitate and sequence organizational, personal/social, and academic needs.

♦ Prepare special needs and multiple-system programming.

♦ Research, evaluate, and document the effectiveness of the transition program.

The Role of the Classroom Teacher

Many educators view meaningful teacher involvement as crucial during the transition stage. When schools are responsive to the needs of the educators who facilitate instruction, the education process, in conjunction with the transition phase, can improve significantly. The staff also needs to be armed with skills that make the transition easier and provide a clear understanding of young adolescents' cognitive, social, and emotional development.

Teachers must recognize middle school as a time of vulnerability, low self-esteem, and delicate egos. These students tend to seek guidance and reassurance. The adolescent's journey through middle school is a road filled with ups and downs. Accompanying students on that journey can challenge even the most effective teacher.

> ## Specific Recommendations
> ## for Middle School Teachers
>
> ◆ Know and understand the physical, social, and emotional characteristics of middle school students.
>
> ◆ Realize that rising middle-level students have a strong need for discipline and guidance.
>
> ◆ Encourage incoming students to do their best work and to avoid peer pressure.
>
> ◆ Accept students for who they are, but give them the support they need.
>
> ◆ Continue to express encouragement, recognition, and praise.
>
> ◆ Demonstrate support by attending events after school.
>
> ◆ Readily assist students with homework or school-related projects.
>
> ◆ Keep students actively engaged in the learning process.
>
> ◆ Expect to be tested; remain calm when challenged.

Sixth-grade students come from a variety of environments, some of which are much smaller than the middle school. Most students may have been taught by only one teacher in each class. To accommodate the differences among beginning middle school students, effective teachers provide numerous opportunities for students to participate in a variety of school-related experiences. They value students regardless of their cultural, racial, or socioeconomic backgrounds and status, and they truly believe that all students can and will learn.

Classroom Teachers as Agents of Socialization

In some respects, teachers have always served as a socializing force in their students' lives. However, the demands on teachers to provide socialization for children have become more encompassing and more complex as varied family backgrounds, cultural diversity, language and learning barriers, and mass media exposure inundate the lives of children. Typically, the younger the student, the greater the expectation that the teacher will function as a socialization force within the school setting. Elementary teachers spend a large portion of time instructing children on the student's role. Good and Brophy (1995) reported that as a child moves through the grades and into high school, socialization is dealt with through administration or other support personnel. However, at every level, "teachers need to develop knowledge and strategies for meeting students' [social-emotional] needs, not just to foster these students' social-emotional adjustment, but also to enable them to make satisfactory academic progress."[10] For this reason, some schools have elected to create school-within-a-school structures that personalize teacher efforts to positively influence the socialization of students as they move through adolescence and into adulthood.

One of the critical times for educators to be sensitive to the socialization of students is during the transition from elementary to middle school. Until recently, small efforts have been made to smooth out this difficult time for early adolescents. In the age of accountability and with several of the standardized tests occurring at the fifth-grade level, this transitional period is receiving more attention. Educators today not only must educate students in reading, writing, and arithmetic, they must also equip them with the motivation and skills to continue learning beyond the walls of the school. As the world becomes increasingly competitive and technology expands our information and communication horizons, students must be more diverse and flexible in their ability to adapt and grow as employees and citizens. In such a rapidly changing society, school remains one of the key socializing forces in American culture. Educators must continue to redefine and expand their roles as they shape young people to meet the needs of tomorrow's world.

References

1. Sack, 2001.
2. Johnston, 2001.
3. Keller, 2000.
4. Olsen, 2000.
5. Archer, 2001.
6. Hatch & Bowers, 2001.
7. Akos, 2002.
8. Eccles et al., 1993.
9. Akos & Martin, 2002.
10. Good and Brophy 2000, p. 184.

References

Akos, P. (2002). Student perceptions of the transition to middle school. *Professional School Counseling, 5*(5), 339–346.

Akos, P. (March/April, 2003). Facilitating successful transitions to middle school: Comprehensive programming for school counselors. *ASCA School Counselor, 14*–18.

Akos, P. & Galassi, J. (2004a). Gender and race as factors in psychosocial adjustment to middle and high school. *The Journal of Educational Research, 98*(2), 102–108.

Akos, P., & Galassi, J. (2004b). Middle and high school transitions as viewed by students, parents, and teachers. *Professional School Counseling, 7*(4), 212–221.

Akos, P. & Martin, M. (2003). Transition groups for preparing students for middle school. *Journal for Specialists in Group Work, 28*(2), 139–154.

Alspaugh, J. W. (1998a). The relationship of school-to-school transitions and school size to drop out rates. *High School Journal, 3,* 154–160.

Alspaugh, J. W. (1998b). Achievement loss associated with the transition to middle school and high school. *Journal of Educational Research, 92*(1), 20–26.

Alpsaugh, J. W. & Harting, R. D. (1995). Transition effects of school grade-level organization on student achievement. *Journal of Research and Development in Education, 28*(3), 145–149.

Alspaugh, J. W., & Harting, R.D. (1997). Effects of team teaching on the transition to middle school. *ERS Spectrum, 15*(1), 9–14.

Anderman, E., & Kimweli, D. (1997). Victimization and safety in schools serving early adolescents. *Journal of Early Adolescence, 17*(4), 408–438.

Anderman, E. M. (1998). The middle school experience: Effects on the math and science achievement of adolescents with LD. *Journal of Learning Disabilities, 31*(2), 128–139.

Anderman, E. M., Maehr, M. L., & Midgley, C. (1999). Declining motivation after the transition to middle school: Schools can make a difference. *Journal of Research and Development in Education, 32,* 131–147.

Anderman, E. M., & Midgley, C. (1996). *Changes in achievement goal orientations after the transition to middle school.* Paper presented at the biennial meeting of the Society for Research on Adolescence, Boston, MA. (ERIC Document Reproduction Service No. ED396226).

Anderman, L. H., & Midgley, C. (1998). *Motivation and middle school students.* (EDO-PS-98-5). Washington, DC: Office of Educational Research and Improvement. (ERIC Document Reproduction Service No. ED421281).

Anderson, L., Jacobs, J., Schramm, S., & Splittgerber, F. (2000). School transitions: Beginning of the end or a new beginning? *International Journal of Educational Research, 33,* 325–339.

Archer, J. (2001). New roles tap expertise of teachers. *Education Week.* Retrieved from the World Wide Web, July 21, 2001.

Arowosafe, D. S., & Irvin, J. L. (1992). Transition to a middle level school: What kids say. *Middle School Journal, 24,* 15–19.

Arth, A. (1990). Moving into the middle school: Concerns of transient students. *Educational Horizons, 68*(2), 105–106.

Bell, J., & Bromnick, R. (2003). The social reality of the imaginary audience: A ground theory approach. *Adolescence, 38,* 205–219.

Berliner, B. (1993, March). *Adolescence, school transitions, and prevention.* Portland, OR: Western Regional Center for Drug-Free Schools and Communities.

Berndt, T., Hawkins, J., & Jiao, Z. (1999). Influences of friends and friendships on adjustment to junior high school. *Merrill-Palmer Quarterly, 45*(1), 13–41.

Blyth, D., Simmons, R., & Carlton-Ford, S. (1983). The adjustment of early adolescents to school transitions. *Journal of Early Adolescence, 3*(1–2), 105–120.

Blos, P. (1970). *The young adolescent: Clinical studies.* New York: Free Press

Bohan-Baker, M., & Little, P. M. (2002). *The transition to kindergarten: A review of current research and promising practices to involve families.* Cambridge, MA: Harvard Family Research Project.

Borgen, W. A. (1995). *Models of adolescent transition.* Greensboro, NC: ERIC Clearinghouse on Counseling and Student Services. (ERIC Digest ED401502).

Bragg, D. D. (1999). *Enhancing linkages to postsecondary education: Helping youths make a successful transition to college.* Berkeley, CA: National Center for Research in Vocational Education.

Brawer, F. B. (1996). *Retention-attrition in the nineties.* Los Angeles: ERIC Clearinghouse for Community Colleges. (ERIC Digest ED393510).

Bronfenbrenner, U. (1979). *The ecology of human development : experiments by nature and design.* Cambridge, MA: Harvard University Press.

Brown, J. M., & Armstrong, R. (1982). The structure of pupils worries during the transition from junior to secondary school. *British Educational Research, 8*(2), 123–131.

Bryk, A., & Thum, Y. (1989). The effects of high school organization on dropping out: An exploratory investigation. *American Educational Research Journal, 26*(3), 353–383.

Burns, Jim. (2002, July). *Addressing needs of young adolescent learners: An integrative perspective on development and practice.* Paper presented at the International Middle Schooling Conference, Adelaide, South Australia.

Burnham, J. F. (2001). *A study of North Carolina principal fellows' perceptions of the adequacy of their administrative training.* Unpublished doctoral dissertation, University of North Carolina, Charlotte.

Carnegie Council on Adolescent Development. (1989). *Turning* points: *Preparing American youth for the 21st century. The report of the Task Force on Education of Young Adolescents.* New York: Author.

Catterall, J. (1995). Risk and resilience in student transitions to high school. *American Journal of Education, 106*(2), 302–335.

Cauce, A., Hannan, K., & Sargeant, M. (1992). Life stress, social support, and locus of control during early adolescence: Interactive effects. *American Journal of Community Psychology, 12*, 353–367.

Chapman, M., & Sawyer, J. (2001). Bridging the gap for students at risk of school failure: A social work-initiated middle to high school transition program. *Children & Schools, 23*(4), 235–241.

Chickering, A. (1993). *Education and identity.* San Francisco: Jossey-Bass.

Chung, H., Elias, M., & Schneider, K. (1998). Patterns of individual adjustment changes during middle school transition. *Journal of School Psychology, 36*, 83–101.

Colorado Department of Education. (2001). *Part C of the Individuals with Disabilities Education Act (IDEA) for infants, toddlers, and their families, year XIII (1999–2000) annual performance report.* Denver, CO: Colorado Department of Education, State Library and Adult Education Office.

Combs, H., & Jurgen, A. (1993). Middle school transition program: Addressing the social side of schooling. *ERS Spectrum, 11*(1), 12–21.

Cooke, G. J. (1995). Choice, not chance: Strengthening school transitions. *Schools in the Middle, 4*(3), 8–12.

Craig, W., Pepler, D., Connolly, J., & Henderson, K. (2001). Developmental context of peer harassment in early adolescence: The role of puberty and the peer group. In S. Graham & J. Juvonen (Eds.), *Peer harassment in school: The plight of the vulnerable and victimized* (pp. 242–261). New York: Guilford Press.

Crockett, L. J., Petersen, A. C., Graber, J. A., Schulenberg, J. E., & Ebata, A. (1989). School transitions and adjustment during early adolescence. *Journal of Early Adolescence, 9,* 181–210.

Cromwell, S. (1998). Where does sixth grade belong? *Education World.* Retrieved January 4, 2003, from http://www.education-world.com.

Decker, J. P. (1997, August). Middle School Brings New Set of Challenges. *Christian Science Monitor.*

Diemert, A. (1992). *A needs assessment of fifth grade students in a middle school.* Acton, MA: Elementary and Early Childhood Education. (ERIC Document Reproduction Service No. ED362332)

Dryfoos, J. (1990). *Adolescents at risk: Prevalence and prevention.* London: Oxford University Press.

Eccles, J. S. (1999). The development of children ages 6–14. *The Future of Children When School Is Out, 9,* 30–44.

Eccles, J., Lord, S., & Roeser, R. Round holes, square pegs, rocky roads, and sore feet: The impact of stage-environment fit on young adolescents' experiences in schools and families. In S. Toth & D. Cicchetti (Eds.), *Adolescence: Opportunities and challenges* (pp. 47–92). Rochester, NY: University of Rochester Press.

Eccles, J. S., Lord, S. E., Roeser, R. W., Barber, B. L., & Hernandez Jozefowicz, D. M. H. (1997). The association of school transitions in early adolescence with developmental trajectories through high school. In J. Schulenberg, J. L. Maggs, & K. Hurrelmann (Eds.), *Health risks and developmental transitions during adolescence* (pp. 283–320). Cambridge: Cambridge University Press.

Eccles, J., & Midgley, C. (1989). Stage/environment fit: Developmentally appropriate classrooms for early adolescents. In R. Ames, & C. Ames (Eds.), *Research on motivation in education* (vol. 3, pp. 139–186). Orlando, FL: Academic Press.

Eccles, J. S., Wigfield, A., Midgley, C., Reuman, D., Mac Iver, D., & Feldlaufer, H. (1993). Negative effects of traditional middle schools on students' motivation. *Elementary School Journal, 93,* 553–574.

Elias, M., Gara, M., Ubriaco, M., et al. (1986). Impact of a preventive social problem solving intervention on children's coping with middle-school stressors. *American Journal of Community Psychology, 14*(3), 259–275.

Feldlaufer, H., Midgley, C., & Eccles, J. (1988). Student, teacher, and observer perceptions of classroom environments before and after the transition to junior high school. *Journal of Early Adolescence, 8,* 133–156.

Felner, R., Jackson, A., Kasak, D., Mulhull, P., Brand, S., & Flowers, N. (1997). The impact of school reform for the middle years: Longitudinal study of a network engaged in Turning Points-based comprehensive school transformation. *Phi Delta Kappan, 78,* 528–532.

Fenzel, L. (1992). The effect of relative age on self-esteem, role strain, GPA, and anxiety. *Journal of Early Adolescence, 12*(3), 253–266.

Ferguson, J., & Bulach, C. (1997). The effect of the "shadow" transition program on the social adjustment of middle school students. *Research in Middle Level Education Quarterly, 20*(2), 1–21.

Ferrandino, V. L. (2002, April). Principal's perspective: Easing the transition. *NAESP Principal Online.* Retrieved January 4, 2003, from http://www.naesp.org.

Flanagan, C., & Eccles, J. (1993). Changes in parents' work status and adolescents' adjustment at school. *Child Development, 64*(1), 246–257.

Forgan, J., & Vaughn, S. (2000). Adolescents with and without LD make the transition to middle school. *Journal of Learning Disabilities, 33*(1), 33–44.

Freshcorn, E. L. (2000). *School transition and students' academic growth in reading and mathematics.* Unpublished doctoral dissertation, University of North Carolina at Charlotte.

Furstenberg, F., Rumbaut, R., & Settersten, R. (2005). Theory, research, and public policy. In F. Furstenberg & R. Settersten (Eds.), *On the frontier of adulthood: Emerging themes and new directions* (pp. 3–25) Chicago: University of Chicago Press.

Gallagher, J., Maddox, M., & Edgar, E. (1984). *Early childhood interagency transition model.* Seattle: Edmark.

Gallagher, V. A. (1994). *Facilitating school transition through effective characterization of skills and collaborative planning: The elementary and middle school child.* Fort Lauderdale, FL: Nova Southeastern University. (ERIC Document Reproduction Service No. ED376927).

Ge, X., Brody, G. H., Conger, R. D., Simons, R. L., & Murry, V. M. (2002). Contextual amplification of pubertal transition effects on deviant peer affiliation and externalizing behavior among African American children. *Developmental Psychology, 38,* 42–54.

Gladieux, L. E., & Swail, W. S. (2000, May). Beyond access. *Phi Delta Kappan, 81*(9), 688–693.

Good, T., & Brophy, J. (1995). *Contemporary educational psychology* (5th ed.). Reading, MA: Addison Wesley Longman.

Grolnick, W., Kurowski, C., Dunlap, K., & Hevey, C. (2000). Parental resources and the transition to junior high. *Journal of Research on Adolescence, 10,* 465–488.

Gutman, L. M., & Midgley, C. (2000). The role of protective factors in supporting the academic achievement of poor African American students during the middle school transition. *Journal of Youth and Adolescence, 29*(2), 223–248.

Hatch, T., & Bowers, J. (2002). The block to build on. *ASCA School Counselor, 39*(5), 12–17.

Hertzog, C., & Morgan, P. (1998). Breaking the barriers between middle school and high school: Developing a transition team for student success. *NASSP Bulletin, 82*(597), 94–98.

Hertzog, J. C. (2002, July 11). Building bridges between middle schools and high schools. Retrieved from http://www. middleweb.com/INCASEbridge.html.

Hirsch, B., & Rapkin, B. (1987). The transition to junior high school: A longitudinal study of self-esteem, psychological symptomology, school life, and social support. *Child Development, 58,* 1235–1243.

Hirsch, B. J., & DuBois, D. L. (1992). The relation of peer social support and psychological symptomatology during the transition to junior high school: A two year longitudinal analysis. *American Journal of Community Psychology, 20,* 333–347.

Isakson, K., & Jarvis, P. (1999). The adjustment of adolescents during the transition into high school: A short-term longitudinal study. *Journal of Youth and Adolescence, 28*(2), 1–26.

Jackson, A. W., & Davis, G. (2000). *Turning Points 2000: Educating adolescents in the 21st century.* New York: Teachers College Press.

Jacobson, L. (1998, March 4). Experts tackle transition to kindergarten. *Education Week, 17*(25), 12.

Jewett, J., Tertell, L., King-Taylor, M., Parker, D., Tertell, L., & Orr, M. (1998). Four early childhood teachers reflect on helping children with special needs make the transition to kindergarten. *Elementary School Journal, 98,* 329–338.

Johnston, R. (2001). Urban renewal. *Education Week, 20*(40), 32–35.

Jones, J. P. (2001). Engineering success through purposeful articulation. In T. S. Dickinson (Ed.), *Reinventing the middle school* (pp. 287–301). New York: RoutledgeFalmer.

Jones, R. M., & Thornberg, H. D. (1984, August). *Environmental mediators of early adolescent self-image.* Paper presented at the annual convention of the American Psychological Association, Toronto, Canada.

Kagan, S., & Neuman, M. (1998). Lessons from three decades of transition research. *Elementary School Journal, 98*(4), 365-79.

Keller, B. (2000). Building on experience. *Education Week.* Retrieved from the World Wide Web, July 21, 2001.

Koenig, L. J., & Gladstone, T. R. G. (1998). Pubertal development and school transitions. *Behavior Modification, 22,* 335–357.

Koizumi, R. (2000). Anchor points in transitions to a new school environment. *Journal of Primary Prevention, 20*(3), 175–187.

Kraft-Sayre, M. E., & Pianta, R. C. (2000). *Enhancing the transition to kindergarten: Linking children, families, and schools.* Charlottesville: University of Virginia Press.

Kurdek, L. A., Fine, M. A., & Sinclair, R. J. (1995). School adjustment in sixth graders: Parenting transitions, family climate, and peer norm effects. *Child Development, 66,* 430–445.

Kurita, J. A., & Janzen, H. L. (1996, August). *The role of social support in mediating school transition stress.* Paper presented at the annual meeting of the American Psychological Association, Toronto, Canada.

LeFrancois, G. (2001). *Of children: An introduction to child and adolescent development* (9th ed.). Belmont, CA: Wadsworth/ Thomson Learning.

Leland-Jones, P. J. (1998). *Improving the transition of sixth-grade students during the first year of middle school through a peer counselor mentor and tutoring program.* Elementary and Early Childhood Education. (ERIC Document Reproduction Service No. ED424911)

Lindsay, D. (1998). Middle-level to high-school transition. *Education Digest, 62*(3), 62–65.

Lord, S. E., & Eccles. J. S. (1994). Surviving the junior high transition. *Journal of Early Adolescence, 14*(2), 162–199.

Lucas, T. (1999). Promoting secondary school transitions for immigrant adolescents. *High School Magazine, 6*(4), 40–41.

Mac Iver, D., & Epstein, J. (1991). Responsive practices in middle grades: Teacher teams, advisory groups, remedial instruction, and school transition programs. *American Journal of Education, 99*(4), 587–622.

Mangione, P. L., & Speth, T. (1998). The transition to elementary school: A framework for creating early childhood continuity through home, school, and community partnerships. *Elementary School Journal, 98*(4), 381–398.

Maute, J. K. (1991). *Transitions concerns of eighth-grade students in six Illinois schools as they prepare for high school.* Unpublished doctoral dissertation, National-Louis University, Evanston, IL.

Mazarr, M. (1999). *Global trends 2005: An owner's manual for the next decade*. New York: St. Martin's Press.

McElroy, C. (2000). Middle school programs that work. *Phi Delta Kappan, 82*(4), 277–279.

McGrady, R. D., & Nestor, P. (2001, December). Raleigh County, West Virginia student transition from elementary to middle school extension program. *Journal of Extension 39*(6).

Meadows, S., & Carmichael, M. (2002, June 3). Meet the gamma girls. *Newsweek, 139*(22), 44–51.

Meekos, D. (1989). *Students' perceptions of the transition to junior high: A longitudinal perspective*. Paper presented at the biennial meeting of the Society for Research Development, Kansas City, MO.

Midgley, C., & Feldlaufer, H. (1987). Students' and teachers' decision-making fit before and after the transition to junior high school. *Journal of Early Adolescence, 7*(2), 225–241.

Midgely, C., Feldlaufer, H., & Eccles, J. (1989). Change in teacher efficacy and student self and task related beliefs during the transition to junior high. *Journal of Educational Psychology, 81,* 247–258.

Milton, T., Schmidtlein, F., Mintrop, H., MacLellan, A., & Pitre, P. (2000, November 16–19). *The high school to college transition: A case study of policies, practices, and K–12 reforms in Maryland*. Paper presented at the annual meeting of the Association for the Study of Higher Education, Sacramento, CA.

Mitchell, M. (1997). *Leaving school: Implementing transition planning; What data and state experiences can tell policy makers and educators*. Washington, DC: Office of Special Education and Rehabilitative Services. (ERIC Document Reproduction Service No. ED408769).

Mitman, A. L., & Packer, M. J. (1982). Concerns of seventh-graders about their transition to junior high school. *Journal of Early Adolescence, 2*(4), 319–338.

Mizelle, N. (1995). *Transition from middle school into high school: The student perspective*. Paper presented at the annual meeting of the American Educational Research Association, San Francisco, CA.

Mizelle, N. (1999). *Helping middle school students make the transition into high school.* (ERIC Document Reproduction Service No. ED432411)

Mizelle, N., & Irvin, J. (2000). Transition from middle school to high school. What research says. *Middle School Journal, 31*(5), 57–61.

Mosely, J., & Lex, A. (1990). Identification of potentially stressful life events experienced by a population of urban minority youth. *Journal of Multicultural Counseling and Development, 18,* 118–125.

Mullins, E. R. (1997). *Changes in young adolescents' self-perceptions across the transition from elementary to middle school.* Unpublished doctoral dissertation, University of Georgia–Athens.

Mullins, E. R., & Irvin, J. L. (2001, January). Transition into middle school. *Middle School Journal.* Retrieved February 5, 2003, from http://www.chapaqua.k12.ny.us.

Mullins, E. R., & Irvin, J. K. (2000). Transition into middle school: What research says. *Middle School Journal, 31*(3), 57–60.

National Middle School Association (NMSA). (1999). *Exemplary middle schools.* (NMSA Research Summary No. 4). Retrieved January 4, 2003, from http://www.nmsa.org.

National Middle School Association. (2002a, March). Parents, schools must take action to help students succeed as they move into middle school. (NMSA/NAESP news release). Retrieved January 4, 2003, from http://www.nmsa.org.

National Middle School Association. (2002b). Supporting students in their transition to middle school: A position paper jointly adopted by the National Middle School Association and the National Association of Elementary School Principals. Retrieved from http://www.nmsa.org/news/transitions.html.

Newman, B. M., Lohman, B. J., Newman, P. R., Myers, M. C., Smith, & V. L. (2000). Experiences of urban youth navigating the transition to ninth grade. *Youth and Society, 31*(4), 387–417.

Oakes, J. (1987). Tracking in secondary schools: A contextual perspective. *Educational Psychologist, 22*(2), 129–153.

Odegaard, S. L., & Heath, J. A. (1992, November) Assisting the elementary school student in the transition to a middle level school. *Middle School Journal, 24*(2), 21–25.

O'Malley, P., & Bachman, J. (1983). Self-esteem: Change and stability between ages 13 and 23. *Developmental Psychology, 19*(2), 257–268.

Osterman, K. (2000). Students' need for belonging in the school community. *Review of Educational Research, 70,* 323–367.

Patterson, P. (1996). Transition skills: Career education and relation social skills. In J. L. Olson, & J. M. Platt (Eds.), *Teaching children and adolescents with special needs* (pp. 367–388). Englewood Cliffs, NJ: Merrill.

Pellegrini, A. D., & Bartini, M. (2000). A longitudinal study of bullying, victimization, and peer affiliation during the transition from primary school to middle school. *American Education Research Journal, 37*(3), 699–725.

Perkins, P. G., & Gelfer, J. I. (1995). Elementary to middle school: Planning for transition. *Clearing House, 68*(3), 171–174.

Perry, K. E., & Weinstein, R. S. (1998). The social context of early schooling and children's school adjustment. *Educational Psychologist, 33*(4), 177–194.

Petersen, A. & Crockett, L. (1985). Pubertal timing and grade effects on adjustment. *Journal of Youth and Adolescence, 14*(3), 191–206.

Petersen, A., Leffert, N., Graham, B., & Alwin, J., et al. (1997). Promoting mental health during the transition into adolescence. In J. Maggs & J. Schulenberg (Eds.), *Health risks and developmental transitions during adolescence.* (pp. 471–497). New York: Cambridge University Press.

Pianta, R. C., Cox, M. J., Taylor, L., & Early, D. (1999). Kindergarten teachers' practices related to transition to school:

Results of a national survey. *Elementary School Journal,* 100(1), 71–86.

Pittman, R., & Haughwout, P. (1987). Influence of high chool size on dropout rate. *Educational Evaluation and Policy Analysis,* 9(4), 337–343.

Pohl, J. (1991). A caring transitions in and out of the middle level school. *Schools in the Middle,* 1(12), 28–29.

Pruitt, D. (1998). *Your child: What every parent needs to know about childhood development from birth to preadolescence.* New York: American Academy of Child and Adolescent Psychiatry.

Queen, J. A. (2002). *Student transitions from middle to high school: Improving achievement and creating a safer environment.* Larchmont, NY: Eye On Education.

Queen, J. A. (2003, September). *ABC Nightly News* [television broadcast]. New York: ABC.

Queen, J. A., & Algozzine. (2006). *Lost in transition.* Charlotte, NC: Writer's Edge Press. In press.

Ramey, S. (1999). Head Start and preschool education: Toward continued improvement. *American Psychologist,* 54(5), 344–346.

Ramey, S. L., & Ramey, C. T. (1994, November). The transition to school: Why the first few years matter for a lifetime. *Phi Delta Kappan,* 76(3), 194–199.

Robertson, Anne S. (2001, October). Transition to Middle School: How Parents Can Help. [Interview with Trevor Kampfi]. *Parent News.* Retrieved January 2, 2003, from http://www.npin.org.

Roderick, M. R. (1993). *The path to dropping out: Evidence for intervention.* Westport, CT: Auburn House.

Roeser, R. W., Eccles, J. S., & Sameroff, A. J. (2000). School as a context of early adolescents' academic and social-emotional development: A summary of research findings. *Elementary School Journal,* 100(5), 443–471.

Roth, M. B. (2004). *A comparison study of elementary to middle school transition program.* Unpublished doctoral dissertation, University of North Carolina–Charlotte.

Ruble, D., & Seidman, E. (1996). Social transition: Windows into social psychological processes. In E. T. Higgins, & A. W. Kruglanski (Eds.), *Social psychology: Handbook of basic principles* (pp. 830–856). New York: Guilford Press.

Sack, J. (2001). Paige releases educational management report, promises accountability. *Education Week.* Retrieved from the World Wide Web, July 21, 2001.

Schave, D., & Schave, B. (1989). *Early adolescence and the search for self: A developmental perspective.* New York: Praeger Publishers.

Schumacher, D. (1998). *The transition to middle school.* (EDO-PS-98-6). Washington, DC: Office of Educational Research and Improvement. (ERIC Document Reproduction Service No. ED422119).

Science and engineering indicators 2002. (n.d.). Retrieved February 11, 2003, from http://www.nsf.gov/sbe/srs/seind02/.

Scott, L., Rock, D., Pollack, J., & Ingles, S. (1995). *Two years later: Cognitive gains and school transitions of NELS; 88 eighth graders.* Washington, DC: National Center for Education Statistics.

Seidman, E., Aber, J., & French, S. (2004). The organization of schooling and adolescent development. In C. Schellenbach & K. Maton (Eds.), *Investing in children, youth, families, and communities: Strengths-based research and policy.* (pp. 233–250). Washington, DC: American Psychological Association.

Seidman, E., Allen, L., Aber, J., Mitchell, C., & Feinman, J. (1994). The impact of school transitions in early adolescence on the self-system and perceived social context of poor urban youth. *Child Development, 65,* 507–522.

Shill, K. (1987). *Precollege guidance and counseling.* (ERIC Digest ED291016). Ann Arbor, MI: ERIC Clearinghouse on Counseling and Personnel Services.

Shoffner, M., & Williamson, R. (2000). Facilitating student transitions into middle school. *Middle School Journal, 31*(4), 47–52.

Simmons, R. (2002). *Odd girl out: The hidden culture of aggression in girls.* New York: Harcourt Brace.

Simmons, R., Black, A., & Zhou, Y. (1991). African-American versus white children and the transition into junior high school. *American Journal of Education, 99*, 481–520.

Simmons, R., & Blyth, D. (1987). *Moving into adolescence: The impact of pubertal change and school context.* Hawthorne, NY: Aldine de Gruyter.

Smetana, J. (1989). Adolescents' and parents' reasoning about actual family conflict. *Child Development, 60*(5), 1052–1067.

Smith, D. R. (1999). *Middle school transition: The strength of ties.* Unpublished doctoral dissertation, Oklahoma State University.

Smith, J. (1997). Effects of eight-grade transition programs on high school retention and experiences. *Journal of Educational Research, 90*(3), 144–152.

Smith, J. B. (1997, January). Effects of eighth grade transition programs on school retention and experiences. *Journal of Educational Research, 90*(3), 144–153.

Spring, J. (2000). *The American school: 1642–2000* (5th ed.). New York: McGraw-Hill.

Tillman, J. D., & Ford, L. (2001). *Analysis of transition services of individualized education programs for high school students with special needs.* Paper presented at the annual meeting of the National Association of School Psychologists, Washington, DC. (ERIC Document Reproduction Service No. ED456608).

Vernon, A., (1993). *Developmental assessment and intervention with children and adolescents.* Alexandria, VA: American Counseling Association.

Waggoner, J. E. (1994). *The relationship between instructional teaming and self-esteem of sixth graders transitioning to a traditional junior high.* Paper presented at a meeting of the Illinois Association of Teachers, Lisle, IL. (ERIC Document Reproduction Service No. 379278).

Wagner, T., & VanderArk, T. (2001). A critical fork in the road. *Education Week*. Retrieved from the World Wide Web, July 21, 2001.

Walsh-Bowers, R. T. (1992). A creative drama prevention program for easing early adolescents' adjustment to school transitions. *Journal of Primary Prevention, 13,* 131–147.

Wampler, R., Fischer, J., Thomas, M., & Lyness, K. (1993). Young adult offspring and their families of origin: Cohesion, adaptability, and addiction. *Journal of Substance Abuse, 5*(2), 195–201.

Wampler, R., Munsch, J., & Adams, M. (2002). Ethic differences in grade trajectories during the transition to junior high. *Journal of School Psychology, 40,* 213–237.

Weldy, G. R. (1991). *Stronger school transitions to improve student achievement: A final report on a three-year demonstration project: Strengthening school transitions for students K–13.* Reston, VA: National Association of Secondary School Principals. (ERIC Document Reproduction Service No. EJ499102).

Weldy, G. R. (1995). Critical transitions. *Schools in the Middle, 4*(3), 3–7.

Wells, M. (1996). *Literacy lost: When students move from a progressive middle school to a traditional high school.* New York: Teachers College Press.

Wentzel, K. (2003). Sociometric status and adjustment to middle school: A longitudinal study. *Journal of Early Adolescence, 23,* 5–28.

Wigfield, A., & Eccles, J. S. (1994, May). Children's competence beliefs, achievement values, and general self-esteem: Change across elementary and middle school. *Journal of Early Adolescence, 14*(2), 107–126.

Wigfield, A., Eccles, J. S., Mac Iver, D., Reoman, D. A., & Midgley, C. (1991). Transitions during early adolescence: Changes in children's domain-specific self-perceptions and general self-esteem across the transition to junior high school. *Developmental Psychology, 27,* 552–565.

Williamson, R., & Johnston, J. (1999). Challenging orthodoxy: An emerging agenda for middle level reform. *Middle School Journal, 30*(4), 10–17.

Wiseman, R. (2002). *Queen bees and wannabes; Helping your daughter survive cliques, gossip, boyfriends, and other realities of adolescence.* New York: Three Rivers Press.

Yee, D., & Flanagan, C. (1985). Family environments and self-consciousness in early adolescence. *Journal of Early Adolescence, 5*(1), 59–68.